# Effective
# Coaching

## Other titles in the Briefcase Books Series include:

*Communicating Effectively* by Lani Arredondo

*Performance Management* by Robert Bacal

*Recognizing and Rewarding Employees*
by R. Brayton Bowen

*Motivating Employees* by Anne Bruce
and James S. Pepitone

*Leadership Skills for Managers* by Marlene Caroselli

*Conflict Resolution* by Daniel Dana

*Managing Teams* by Lawrence Holpp

*Hiring Great People* by Kevin C. Klinvex,
Matthew S. O'Connell, and Christopher P. Klinvex

*Empowering Employees* by Kenneth L. Murrell and
Mimi Meredith

*The Manager's Guide to Business Writing*
by Suzanne D. Sparks

*Skills for New Managers* by Morey Stettner

---

To learn more about titles in the Briefcase Books series go to
**www.briefcasebooks.com**
You'll find the tables of contents, downloadable sample chapters, information on the authors, discussion guides for using these books in training programs, and more.

# Effective
# Coaching

**Marshall J. Cook**

## McGraw-Hill

New York  San Francisco  Washington, D.C.  Auckland  Bogotá
Caracas  Lisbon  London  Madrid  Mexico City  Milan
Montreal  New Delhi  San Juan  Singapore
Sydney  Tokyo  Toronto

# McGraw-Hill

*A Division of The McGraw-Hill Companies*

Copyright © 1999 by The McGraw-Hill Companies, Inc. All rights reserved. Printed in the United States of America. Except as permitted under the United States Copyright Act of 1976, no part of this publication may be reproduced or distributed in any form or by any means, or stored in a database or retrieval system, without the prior written permission of the publisher.

9 0 DOC/DOC    0 3

ISBN 0-07-071864-4

**Library of Congress Cataloging-in-Publication Data**

Cook, Marshall, 1944-
      Effective Coaching / Marshall J. Cook
          p.    cm.
      A Briefcase Book
      ISBN 0-07-071864-4
      1. Employees—Counseling of. 2. Employee motivation.
      3. Mentoring in business. 4. Supervision of employees.
      HF5549.5.C8C66 1999
      658.3/1244 21                                              98041551

*This is a CWL Publishing Enterprises Book, developed and produced for McGraw-Hill by CWL Publishing Enterprises, John A. Woods, President. For more information, contact CWL Publishing Enterprises, 3010 Irvington Way, Madison, WI 53713-3414, www.execpc.com/cwlpubent. Robert Magnan served as editor. Page layout by Cleveland Publishing Services, Madison, WI. For McGraw-Hill, the sponsoring editor was Catherine Schwent, the publisher was Jeffrey Krames, the editing supervisor was John M. Morriss, and the production supervisor was Suzanne W. B. Rapcavage.*

*Printed and bound by R. R. Donnelley & Sons*

McGraw-Hill books are available at special quantity discounts to use as premiums and sales promotions, or for use in corporate training programs. For more information, please write to the Director of Special Sales, McGraw-Hill, Professional Publishing, Two Penn Plaza, New York, NY 10121-2298. Or contact your local bookstore.

 This book is printed on recycled, acid-free paper containing a minimum of 50% recycled de-inked fiber.

# Contents

gratis

114053

# Preface

As I wrote this book on coaching, I kept thinking about my Dad. He taught me how to hit a baseball, shoot a jump shot, bait and set a hook, cook stew in a campfire—stuff you can't get out of a book. He didn't teach me to love these things. That just happened.

His method was strictly hands on (mine) and hands off (his).

To teach me to hit, for example, he put the bat in my hands and pitched to me endlessly. Only now do I realize how tired he must have been and how much patience the practices required of him. He offered few suggestions. Mostly I remember his soft grunt of exertion as he threw and his joyful "Atta boy!" on the rare occasions when I connected.

His advice wasn't original. "Keep your eye on the ball," he'd say. Easy to say, but hard to do when you're a scared kid. He knew that: "It only takes one. Make him pitch to you. Pick one out."

I can summarize his advice on fishing in one compact sentence: "Keep the tip up." The rest I learned by watching and doing.

I remember one particular fishing trip, when I was perhaps eight. We were in a row boat on Lake Arrowhead, in the San Bernardino Mountains of southern California, just at dawn. The water was still and black. He had rigged my pole and let me bait up and cast and was getting his own pole ready when I felt the terrifying mystery of a fish, far down in the water, bumping up against my bait.

"Wait," he murmured, "Wait," as the tip of the pole dipped once, twice, then a third time, almost taking the pole out of my hands.

"Now!" he said, and I set the hook, imitating his fierce, two-handed motion.

He made no move to take the pole from me. This was my fish to catch or to lose. "Keep the tip up," he said calmly.

But his hands were shaking with excitement as he put the net into the water and waited for me to bring the fish, head up, into the opening.

Miraculously, he lifted my fish into the boat, the early sun glittering the scales. He deftly broke the fish's neck so it wouldn't suffer. Then he took out the tape measure.

"I make it thirteen and a quarter," he said, holding my fish up, just as the nurse in the maternity ward might hold up a newborn.

I heard him tell the story in the village later that day, about how his kid caught this huge rainbow trout before he could even get his line in the water. I heard him tell that story for the rest of his life.

I've had lots of other coaches—in athletics, in school, and on the job. Some were good, some awful, a few great. My Dad was my first and best coach.

I don't play baseball or basketball anymore, and I haven't been fishing or camping lately. But I still try to apply what he taught me about patience and trust every day of my life.

In this book, you'll learn how to apply good coaching methods in the workplace, helping employees achieve high performance by seeking commitment rather than control and results rather than somebody to blame.

As we describe the main functions of the coach in the workplace and examine the structure of an effective coaching session, we stress coaching on the run, where you'll really do your best work. Two simple principles guide us: KYHO (keep your hands off) and PSA (positive, specific action).

We'll discuss the pitfalls to good coaching and help you understand the best ways to avoid them.

By studying worker motivations beyond the paycheck, you'll learn to challenge employees to achieve and learn. You'll also learn to communicate effectively, by giving clear instructions and by asking effective questions and hearing the answers.

You'll learn to use intrinsic, intangible reward—ownership, mastery, and growth—to spur peak performance while fostering independence and initiative.

The bonus principles described in Chapter 17 will help your coaching and all other aspects of your life—because coaching will become a vital part of your life and give you skills to apply outside the workplace as well.

You ready, coach? Let's get going.

I'd love to hear about your coaching experiences and will of course try to answer any questions you might have. Contact me at marshall.cook@ccmail.adp.wisc.edu or at mjc903@aol.com.

## Acknowledgments

I have long been interested in coaching but didn't think to write a book about it until John Woods of CWL Publishing Enterprises approached me. He worked with me to develop the manuscript, and he along with Robert Magnan, also of CWL, edited and turned my manuscript into the book you now hold. I also want to thank you for picking me as a coach to help you learn about coaching.

## Special Features

The idea behind the books in the Briefcase Series is to give you practical information written in a friendly person-to-person style. The chapters are short, deal with tactical issues, and include lots of examples. They also feature numerous boxes designed to give you different types of specific information. Here's a description of the boxes you'll find in this book.

 These boxes do just what they say: give you tips and tactics for being a smart manager and coach.

 These boxes provide warnings for where things could go wrong.

 Here you'll find how-to hints to make your job as a coach easier.

 Every subject has its special jargon and terms. These boxes provide definitions of these concepts.

 Want to know how others have done it? Look for these boxes.

 Here you'll find specific procedures you can follow to get results.

 How can you make sure you won't make a mistake? You can't, but these boxes will give you practical advice on how to minimize the possibility.

## About the Author

Marshall Cook is a professor in the Division of Continuing Studies at the University of Wisconsin–Madison. He teaches workshops, seminars, and courses on writing and on time and stress management and media relations. He consults with businesses and government agencies on organization management topics, and is a frequent speaker at conferences nationwide.

For eight years he was chairman of the Language Arts Division of Solano Community College, Suisun City, California, and for two years served as chairman of the Communication Programs Department of the University of Wisconsin–Madison Outreach.

He has also run his own freelance writing and consulting business for 19 years. His published books include: *Slow Down and Get More Done* (1993), *The 10-Minute Guide to Motivating People* (1997) and *Streetwise Time Management* (1999).

Marshall edits *Creativity Connection*, a newsletter for writers and independent publishers, and has published articles in hundreds of regional and national magazines. For two years he served as Editorial Advisor for *Business Age* magazine, Milwaukee, Wisconsin.

# The Goals of Good Coaching

The four district managers aren't getting their phone messages fast enough. They're upset about it, and they say they're losing orders because of it.

All fingers point at Sonya. Incoming calls are routed to her phone, and her voice mail backs everybody up. You've got to solve the problem. What's your first move?

We'll come back to this situation after you've learn about the goals of good coaching and how management by coaching will help you get the information you need.

## Are You Wasting Your Most Valuable Resource?

According to a recent survey by Market Facts' TeleNation, more than 90 percent of the employees polled believe they have good ideas about how their companies could be run more successfully. However, only 38 percent think their employers would be interested in hearing those ideas, making employees' ideas a most wasted resource.

Do workers feel comfortable coming to you with suggestions? Maybe your door is always open, but is anybody walking through it?

## An Accessibility Quotient Quiz

Your "Accessibility Quotient" is your openness to input from your staff. How would your workers respond to the following statements? Answer "yes" or "no" as you think they'd *really* respond, not as you'd like them to.

My boss

1. asks for my opinion frequently.
2. listens to my suggestions.
3. takes my ideas seriously.
4. values my opinion.
5. checks with me before making a decision that affects my work.
6. would defend me in a meeting of supervisors.
7. explains goals clearly when giving me a new project.
8. welcomes my questions about an ongoing project.
9. gives me latitude in deciding how to carry out a project.
10. saves criticism for one-on-one sessions.

### What Your Responses Tell You About Your Management Style

Did you rack up seven or more positive responses on the Accessibility Quotient Quiz? If so, you're already exhibiting many of the attributes of a good coach. One of the main goals of management by coaching is to create an atmosphere in which employees are willing and able to share their ideas with their superior.

Getting fewer than seven positive responses doesn't mean you're a failure, however. A low score just means you've got some work to do. (That low score may also indicate that you're more honest and self-critical than most managers.)

Let's look at each statement and what it indicates about your working relationship with your employees.

**1. My boss asks for my opinion frequently.** The people who work with you already know you don't have all the answers. So when you ask for an employee's input, three good things happen, before you even get an answer: (1) you show your respect for the employee, (2) you show that you don't think you have a corner on wisdom, and (3) you open yourself to an opportunity to get valuable information. "How do you think we should handle it?" can be one of the best things you ever say to an employee.

**2. My boss listens to my suggestions.** Asking is

> ⚠️ **CAUTION!**
> ## Watch Out for Attitude
> If you hesitated before answering some of these questions, you may be revealing a lack of awareness of workers' attitudes. If so, pay particular attention to tips in this book on becoming sensitive to employee feedback, which includes written and oral messages, of course, and also body language and other indicators.

only half of the process. Listening is the other half.

Give employees your full attention. Indicate by word and gesture that you're taking in what they say. Ask questions. Respond honestly.

**3. My boss takes my ideas seriously.** You say, "Uh-huh. That's ... interesting."

The employee hears, "Thanks for nothing. Now we'll do it my way."

You won't necessarily agree with employees' perspectives, and you may not act on their suggestions. But if they offer the input sincerely, you should take it seriously.

If you think an idea has merit, say so. If you think it's flawed, say why.

> ⚠️ **CAUTION!**
> ## Ask Their Opinions
> Unfortunately, many employees go to work every day without ever being asked for their opinions. They won't expect you to want that input unless you ask for it, and they may not trust you when you do. Be patient, walk your talk, and you'll win their trust and candor.

Discuss ideas, not personalities. Never allow the discussion to become a battle between "your idea" and "their idea" or a contest with a winner and a loser.

**4. My boss values my opinion.** You show that you value an opinion by listening to it, by taking it seriously, and by rewarding it. Most businesses reward results—jobs successfully completed, goals reached, bottom lines enriched—if they reward employee performance at all. Appreciation should begin much earlier in the process, when you're looking for hard work, cooperation, and creative input.

It takes courage and initiative for an employee to speak up. Reward that courage through your words and deeds. Questions and suggested alternatives are positive contributions, not threats.

**5. My boss checks with me before making a decision that affects my work.** You're the boss. You make the decisions. But when a decision affects working conditions, you should talk it over with employees and get their input first—not only to show that you respect them, but also to help you make the best decision.

**6. My boss would defend me in a meeting of supervisors.** Are you willing to go to bat for your employees, to fight for them, to defend them from unjust attacks, and to take your share of the blame when something goes wrong?

Would your workers say that you're a "stand-up boss"? There's no higher praise they can give you.

**7. My boss explains goals clearly when giving me a new project.** Employees are no better at reading your mind than you are at reading theirs. When you give them a task, do you take the time to outline in clear, simple terms exactly what they should accomplish? An employee who understands the overall purpose of her work will do a better job and feel better about doing it. And you'll prevent costly mistakes down the line.

---

**MISTAKE PROOFING**

**Prepare and Be Clear**

If you've ever tried to explain anything to anybody, you know how difficult it can be to say something clearly and simply. Prepare yourself before you give instructions. Think the job through, and anticipate potential snags and confusion.

---

**8. My boss welcomes my questions about an ongoing project.** "Do you understand?"

## Giving Instructions

Be careful about the amount and nature of the directions you give. Make sure that directions are appropriate to the situation.

"I want you to increase sales by five percent in the next quarter" may be enough of a charge for a trusted salesperson with experience, product knowledge, and the necessary authority to do the job (for example, the ability to negotiate the terms of an offer or to spend up to a set amount for increased promotion). However, "I want you to make 30 copies of each of these handouts, and I want you to do it by taking them down to the copy machine and setting the counter to 30 and feeding in the originals one at a time" is probably a whole lot more instruction than most people need—or appreciate.

When most folks ask that question, they expect a quick "Yes" (in the same way most of us expect a perfunctory "Fine, thanks" when we ask, "How are you?").

Employees' questions will seem like interruptions and irritations—unless you train yourself to expect and even welcome them. Questions are often the only way you really know what an employee has heard and understood. Employees willing to ask you a question now—knowing that they won't be penalized for showing "ignorance"—will do a better job.

**9. My boss gives me latitude in deciding how to carry out a project.**

Explain goals clearly and precisely. Answer all questions. But don't always spell out exactly how those goals should be reached. Whenever possible, leave room for creativity and initiative.

**10. My boss saves criticism for one-on-one sessions.**

Praise in public, criticize in private—not so that people will think you're a nice person, but because it works. Public criticism engenders defensiveness and anger—in the employee criticized and in everybody else within earshot. Criticism in private, delivered decisively but respectively, has a much better chance of getting you what you want—improved performance.

## The Benefits of Good Coaching

Effective coaching moves an employee from WIIFM (What's in it for me?) to WIIFU (What's in it for us?). It enables you, as the coach, to reap specific benefits from your efforts. Let's look at the benefits you can derive from being a successful coach.

### Helps Develop Employees' Competence

Watch a loving parent initiate a child into the mysteries of riding a two-wheeled bicycle. First the parent instructs the child and then shows how it is done. But at some point the kid has to climb on that bicycle and ride it alone.

> **Smart Managing**
>
> **Success Builds on Itself**
> The goal of good coaching isn't just to help employees reach a certain performance level. It's important to realize that one success engenders another and instills the self-confidence that leads to high levels of motivation and performance in many tasks.

Now imagine that you're the loving parent, running beside the wobbling bike, shouting encouragement, your hand first tightly clutching the handle bars and then gradually loosening your grip until finally, your heart in your throat, you let go, launching your child into the world.

Now imagine that you're the child on the bike. You're terrified and exhilarated, concentrating on keeping the pedals pumping and the bike from dumping. But at some point—hours, days, or maybe even weeks later—you realize that the balancing act, at first seemingly impossible, has become second nature. You don't have to think about riding the bike; you can just do it—and enjoy it.

You no longer need your coach. And that's the point. Good coaches keep creating situations where they're no longer needed.

### Helps Diagnose Performance Problems

If employees aren't performing at peak efficiency, you have to figure out the reason. Too often, getting input from the people closest to the job, the employees themselves, is overlooked.

A good coach first asks for employee input, then listens to it. By doing so, you're more likely to make the right diagnosis, and you're also more likely to get worker cooperation in arriving at a solution. If employees feel empowered to solve the problem, they'll solve it.

> **Keep an Open Mind**
>
> **Smart Managing**
>
> When you seek causes for problems, be ready to abandon your assumptions. You may assume, for example, that the person closest to the origin of the problem is responsible for it. But if you keep an open mind, you might find the bottleneck elsewhere, perhaps even at the supervisory level.

### Helps Correct Unsatisfactory or Unacceptable Performance

Once you've found the source of the problem, you can decide how to correct it. Here again, don't overlook a rich potential source of solutions—the employees themselves. Brainstorm with a group of employees and let them help you evaluate potential actions.

### Helps Diagnose a Behavioral Problem

Behavioral problems are sticky territory. Performance is at least somewhat objective. You can count outputs and actions taken, and you can compare today's performance with yesterday's and mine with yours. But evaluating

> **Deal with the Problem**
>
> **Smart Managing**
>
> "Don't shoot all the dogs," Paul Newman as Hud Bannon advises, "just because one of them's got rabies."
>
> If you determine that the problem lies with one employee's phone-answering performance, don't send all the employees to phone-answering school. Work—or arrange to have someone else work—with the specific employee on the specific problem. In this way, you won't be wasting anybody else's time, and you won't create resentment.

employees' behavior is often a matter of assessing attitude and demeanor.

You may think that some employees spend way too much time chatting about personal matters when they should be tending to business. But how much time is "too much"? Others may view your workplace and comment on the friendliness and seeming cooperation among staff members. You're on much safer ground when you confine employee evaluations to outputs you can measure. If those chatty employees are getting their work done, if that work is satisfactory, and if their conversation isn't bothering anybody else, the "problem" may be nothing more than your own irritation. (You might even be a little jealous, feeling that you don't even have time to breathe, much less chat, during the workday.)

Behavioral guidelines are often vague, but the stakes can be staggeringly high—in lawsuits and grievances alleging discrimination, for example.

Using the basic principles of good coaching is even more important in these situations. Involve relevant employees in defining the situation and in determining whether behaviors are getting in the way of performance. Keep an open mind, and keep your assumptions to yourself. Be willing to explain any decisions you may make, along with options for appeal to a higher level.

### Smart Managing

### Make Them Aware

It's not unusual for employees to complain that other employees are bothering them. When this happens, those doing the bothering are usually unaware of how their behavior is affecting others. Often the situation can be improved by sensitively informing the offending individuals how others feel and by making suggestions on how to make improvements.

## Helps Correct Unsatisfactory or Unacceptable Behavior

Three of the four members of your office staff are chatting happily; the fourth is seething. Patti considers the talk to be petty gossip. It's distracting and annoying, she tells you, especially when she's on the phone with a potential client. She feels that her own job performance is suffering. She also lets you know, without saying so directly, that she doesn't see how the others could possibly be getting their work done with all that conversation. Her solution? She wants permission to bring in her CD player so that she can use music to screen out the noise.

How about it, coach? Do you let Patti bring in her CDs—which may or may not improve her work performance but will surely give her a clear "victory" over the other three? Do you give Patti a pair of earplugs and tell her to tough it out? Do you send a memo to all personnel outlining guidelines for maintaining a "professional atmosphere" in the office?

You might come up with a list of possible solutions (including, of course, the ever-popular "do nothing, and hope it blows over"). No matter how long that list is, you won't come up with one suggestion that doesn't make somebody mad.

There's a better way, coach: huddle up with the players and talk it through. You'll learn how to conduct these sessions, step by step, in later chapters. You'll get the results you want—and you'll save time doing it.

## Fosters Productive Working Relationships

"Works well with others." When I was growing up, teachers let parents know on report cards how we were getting along with the other kids. We went to school to learn social skills (wait your turn, share your crayons, no kicking, and so on) as well as academic subjects.

In the office, people are not graded on their social skills—at least not in so many words. Companies set performance objectives, but still talk about intangibles like "attitude" and whether or not an employee is a "team player." They still want people to "work well with others"; they just call it something different.

As you apply the techniques of good coaching in the workplace, you'll notice better performance from your employees and also employees helping each other. When you set the example as head coach, people take the hint and start coaching each other to higher levels of performance. You couldn't order them to do it, but it can happen without your saying a thing.

### Focuses on Providing Appropriate Guidance and Counseling

Nobody's suggesting that you provide therapy. In fact, if you tried, you'd get in more trouble than you can imagine. But as a coach, you can and should be a mentor for any worker who seeks or is open to your guidance. You're dealing with human beings, not components in a piece of equipment. Employees want a lot more than a paycheck at the end of the week and a performance evaluation at the end of the year. They think about their careers

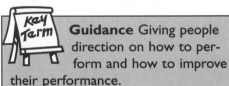

**Guidance** Giving people direction on how to perform and how to improve their performance.

**Counseling** Helping employees become more aware of their behavior, how it might cause problems on the job, and how to turn things around.

within and without the organization. They deserve to know the unwritten rules, the stuff that never shows up in the handbook. Who's there to guide them through the rapids? Nobody but you, coach.

### Provides Opportunities for Conveying Appreciation

Many of us have a hard time saying "Thank you" or "Good job." We lack formal occasions and established patterns for giving praise, and we find it difficult to ad-lib.

Coaching provides natural opportunities to praise good work and strong effort

### Fosters Self-coaching Behaviors

As you become an effective coach, you'll find that employees will become more and more competent. When you coach an employee through a challenge, you teach that employee to figure out how to deal with similar problems in the future.

Remember: your role isn't just about getting specific tasks completed. It's about creating more competent and committed employees who have the ability to add ever-higher levels of value to the organization.

### Improves Employee Performance and Morale

Call it "morale." Call it "self-esteem." Call it whatever you want. How your staff members feel about themselves and their roles in the workplace makes a big difference in their performances.

Coaching them with respect does a lot to improve that morale. And it also affects their performance. By allowing employees to take responsibility and initiative for their work, you'll improve their morale in ways no seminar, pep talk, or self-help book ever could.

This tenth point, then, is the culmination of the first nine. As you increase performance through coaching, you also improve morale. Your ability to coach effectively communicates to employees that you care about them and are committed to helping them improve. This can translate into their being committed and excited about their work. And this naturally leads to higher performance and higher morale. In other words, all these actions go together, and coaching is the method that makes it happen.

## Meanwhile, Back at the Message Board...

Let's go back to the story at the beginning of this chapter. Along with complaints from the managers that they aren't getting their phone messages quickly enough, you've heard a few comments from customers—not complaints, exactly, just offhand statements about a call not returned, an order not routed to the right department, a question lost in the shuffle.

You need to act decisively and promptly. You want to improve the message system, of course, and you also want to retain the trust and confidence of your managers. What are your options?

1. Send a memo to everybody in the office outlining proper phone procedures. That way, Sonya will get the message

without feeling singled out. Besides, other folks might benefit from the reminder.

2. Warn Sonya about the problem, give her three months to shape up, and put a note in her personnel file. To hell with her feelings. She's falling down on the job, and she needs to shape up.

3. Send Sonya to a workshop on telephone technique. She's probably trying to do a good job. Maybe she just doesn't know how.

4. Investigate a new voice-mail system. By spending a few bucks, you may be able to fix the problem without upsetting Sonya.

5. Do nothing. It's been especially hectic lately. The situation might work itself out when things simmer down. Besides, Sonya has made no secret about being unhappy with her job. Maybe she'll take a lateral transfer soon.

So what's your call, coach?

"None of the above." You don't know enough about the problem to create a solution. You need more information—and one of the best sources of that information is sitting out in the front office right now, fuming about how mean everybody's been to her lately.

In later chapters, we'll discuss the best ways to get that information. For now, let's listen in on a conversation that will give you a good sense of how a skillful coach might handle the situation.

**You:** "I'd like to take a look at the way we handle phone messages. Can you give me a few minutes to explain the system to me?"

**Sonya:** "Sure. Now's fine."

(Notice how cooperative employees are when you get to write both sides of the dialog! Sonya explains how messages get bumped to her when a manager doesn't pick up after three rings. If she's on another call, voice mail picks up immediately. If she's out of the office, and nobody catches the call, the phone rings three more times before voice mail takes the message.)

**You:** "So, in that case, a caller has to wait through six rings before getting any response?"

**Sonya:** "Yep. But they'll hear a click after three rings when the call transfers. They should know what's going on."

**You:** "Do we have any way of knowing if somebody hangs up before the sixth ring?"

**Sonya:** "Not that I know of. I can call the company and check."

**You:** "That would be great. Let me know what you find out. Now, suppose the call kicks over to you, and you get it on the first ring."

**Sonya:** (shaking her head vigorously): "I never pick up on the first ring."

> **⚠ CAUTION!**
>
> **Avoid Sarcasm**
>
> In a conversation like this, there may be a tendency for an employee to get sarcastic. It's important not to respond negatively to this. You should also not become sarcastic in response, or neither of you will take the conversation seriously and your respect for each other may be undermined. Instead, ignore the sarcasm and keep the conversation focused on information gathering and problem solving.

**You:** "Why is that?"

**Sonya:** "Because if it's one of those stupid computer solicitations, they usually hang up before the second ring."

**You:** "I didn't know that."

**Sonya:** "Oh, yeah. The computer dials ten numbers at a time. When one picks up, they hang up on the other nine."

**You:** (guiding the conversation back on course): "So, the phone rings five times before you pick up, right?"

**Sonya:** "Yeah. Then I take a message."

**You:** "Right. And what happens if you don't pick up after five rings?"

**Sonya:** "They get my voice mail."

**You:** "Right. How often do you harvest the messages?"

**Sonya:** "I always check right away if I've been out of the office."

**You:** "Excellent. Then what do you do with the messages?"

**Sonya:** "I stick them on the message board, behind the old copier."

**You:** "That copier hasn't worked for eight months."

**Sonya:** "Right."

**You:** "So, that's what that board's for."

**Sonya:** "It's been there for five years."

**You:** "No kidding?"

**Sonya:** "You and the managers. They act like they don't know what it is, either."

**You:** "How's that?"

**Sonya:** "Phone messages really pile up over there. Randy [a manager] only comes in for his messages once a day, after lunch. Sometimes he'll have 15 or 20 up there."

**You:** "Any ideas on how we might get things moving faster?"

**Sonya:** "If you mean that I should carry the messages down to their offices for them every time, I can tell you right now, I wouldn't get anything else done if I did that."

**You:** "I wouldn't even suggest such a thing. Any other ideas?"

**Sonya:** "Why don't I just put the messages in everybody's mailboxes? They're right next door."

**You:** "How often do they check the mailboxes?"

**Sonya:** "Good point. Most of them only go in there once a day, after I sort the mail."

**You:** "Any other ideas?"

**Sonya:** "Yeah. Why don't you kick a little butt and tell the managers to check their messages more often?"

**You:** "I don't know about kicking butt, but I will see if I can get people to check more often."

**Sonya:** "Maybe we could move the message board to a better place—like right behind the coffee pot and the microwave."

**You:** "Everybody would see messages there, all right."

**Sonya:** "Yeah, and everybody else will see how Randy lets his messages stack up."

**You:** "Let's give it a try. Maybe we can even get Randy to check more often. Can you write up a work order to have it moved?"

**Sonya:** "Sure, but I'm not sure how much good it will do. The folks in maintenance don't take these requests too seriously."

**You:** "Yeah, I know. However, I'll make a call over there and emphasize the importance of taking care of this now. After it's been up about a week, let's get together so you can bring me up to date on how well it's working. Maybe we could kick around some other ideas for improving the system."
**Sonya:** "Sure."
**You:** "Thanks."

That's how the dialog *might* go. Still, however it proceeds, you can expect the interchange to be productive when employees trust you enough to express themselves freely with the expectation that you're there to help. And it's likely that you'll make progress toward a solution even if you don't solve the problem outright.

And that's what this book is all about—helping you achieve peak employee performance through good coaching. Read on.

## The Coach's Checklist for Chapter 1

❏ If you're not developing your people, your wasting your most valuable resource.

❏ How accessible are you? If you didn't take the accessibility quiz, go back and do it now.

❏ Coaching is good for employees, and it's good for managers as well. By coaching you build the relationships that will result in continuously improved performance for you and your employees.

# The Attributes of a Good Coach

Clarke Stallworth glowered at the room full of skeptical editors. "I used to be really tough." Then the former managing editor of the Birmingham, Alabama News grinned.

"When a reporter handed me a story," he said, beginning to pace, "I knew what was wrong with it and I fixed it! I tore it to shreds!" Stallworth picked up a copy of the local newspaper and ripped it into long, ragged strips.

"And they hated me for it!" he thundered, wadding the torn shreds of paper into a ball.

He kept grinning as he described his conversion from hard-bitten editor who "fixed" copy to hard-driving coach who helped reporters improve their own copy and, in the process, become better writers. He continued working the wad of newsprint as he talked.

"The copy isn't what it's all about," he said, his eyes moving from face to face in the audience. "The reporter's what it's all about."

His eyes settled on an especially skeptical editor, who had been leaning back in his chair, arms folded, head tilted.

"How long do your reporters stay with you?" Stallworth asked.

Uncomfortable at being singled out, the editor shifted in his chair. "Eighteen months, maybe," he answered. Around the room, heads nodded.

"You just get 'em broke in good," Stallworth said, "and you gotta start all over with a new one, right?"

"Well, yeah," the editor agreed.

"You know why your reporters leave you?"

The editor shrugged. "The pay stinks," he said, provoking laughter and more head-nodding around the room.

"The pay stinks everywhere," Stallworth said. "Reporters leave you because they aren't learning anything from you. They aren't getting any better. Keep teaching them and they'll stay longer."

Still gently kneading the wad of newsprint, Stallworth explained the difference between an editor and a coach.

"The editor takes the copy from the reporter and fixes it. The story then belongs to the editor, not the reporter. The editor stays mad at the 'stupid' reporter, and the reporter stays mad at the 'pigheaded' editor.

"The coach sits down with the reporter and asks two questions: 'What's good about this story?' and 'How could it be better?' By the time the reporter answers those questions, she's ready to fix the story herself. She's learned how to write better, and the story is still hers. She's proud of it.

"Instead of being ripped up, the story comes out whole," Stallworth concluded. Then he carefully opened up the ball of newspaper he'd been holding. It had been restored to a full page.

"There's nothing magic about it," he concluded, the grin splitting his face. "It's just plain commonsense."

## Characteristics of a Good Coach

A good coach is positive, enthusiastic, supportive, trusting, focused, goal-oriented, knowledgeable, observant, respectful, patient, clear, and assertive. Let's look at how each characteristic comes into play in the workplace.

**A good coach is** *positive*. Your job is *not* correcting mistakes, finding fault, and assessing blame. Instead, your function is achieving productivity goals by coaching your staff to peak performance.

Ken knows he's supposed to get his monthly performance reports in by the tenth of the month, but he never gets them done until the fourteen or fifteenth. You've talked to him about the problem several times, but Ken still doesn't get the reports in on time.

Try the positive approach. It's the difference between saying, "Get those reports in by the tenth" and asking, "What do you need to do differently to get your monthly performance reports in by the tenth?"

The first statement reaps resentment and excuses—but no improvement in performance. You continue thinking of Ken as a problem; Ken goes on thinking of you as a jerk.

The second approach can get you what you want—the reports turned in on time. And you've got a shot at winning the bonus prize—a worker with a more cooperative attitude and improved time management skills to apply to the next task.

## Coach's Questions

One of the keys to effective coaching is asking questions rather than providing answers. But the specific questions, and the order in which you ask those questions, make the difference between success and failure. Here's an effective one-two punch for many situations: (1) What's good about it? And (2) How could it be better?

This approach stresses the positive, building on the work's strengths, rather than focusing on its weaknesses. But can the person who just finished the work really analyze its strengths and weaknesses?

Nobody knows them better.

**A good coach is** *enthusiastic*. As a leader, you set the tone. Your attitude is catching. Project gloom and doom, and you'll get gloom and doom back from your staff. If you concoct reasons why things won't work out, your staff will never disappoint you—things won't work out.

Bring positive energy to every encounter. *Don't* play it cool.

**A good coach is** *supportive.* Being supportive means a lot more than providing an encouraging word and a pat on the back. Your job as coach is to get workers what they need to do their jobs well, including tools, time, instruction, answers to questions, and protection from outside interference.

To lead, you must serve, anticipating needs and preventing problems from happening.

**A good coach is** *trusting.* Do you expect workers to be infallible, performing their jobs on time, every time, with no errors?

Of course you don't. Everybody makes mistakes. Employees have personal crises that interfere with their work. They have good days and not-so-good days, times of peak efficiency and times when they slide into a stupor. Your staff members are human, a characteristic they share with their coach.

Do you trust employees to be conscientious, to tell the truth, and to give a reasonable day's work for a day's pay?

You'd better. You shouldn't hire someone unless you're willing to extend the person that kind of trust. Most people are conscientious and honest, with an inherent desire to do their jobs well. And when they see you applying high standards to your own conduct, they'll be even more likely to do the same. Tell them what to do, and then clear out and let them do it. Don't let them catch you looking over their shoulders.

**A good coach is** *focused.* The temptation can be overwhelming. While you've got the employee in your office, discussing a current performance challenge, why not discuss the other problems you've been meaning to discuss for weeks?

Don't do it. Don't take that poor worker on a guided tour of your personal Hall of Horrors.

Effective communication is specific and focused. Deal in particulars. Keep the task manageable. You're far more likely to get action if that employee leaves your office focused on resolving the issue at hand.

**A good coach is** *goal-oriented.* "Why does she want me to do that?" If you leave workers pondering that question after you've explained an assignment, you've only done half the job.

**The Positive Approach**

*For Example*

Here's how you might use the positive approach with Ken to get a positive outcome.

**You:** "We really need those reports by the tenth. Any later than that, and everything gets jammed up in personnel, and some folks might not get paid on time. Nobody wants that. What do you think we need to do differently to get the reports in on time?"

**Ken:** "I just need to get started on them earlier."

**You:** "When do you start them now?"

**Ken:** "First of the month, as soon as I get the evaluations from the unit chairs."

**You:** "Is everybody getting those to you on time?"

**Ken:** "Pretty much. Except for Toby. His comes in by the third."

**You:** "I can talk to Toby if you want."

**Ken:** "No. That's not why my reports are late. No matter when I get the evaluations, I always stick them in a drawer and leave them there until the afternoon of the ninth. I figure I'll work straight through and get them done, but it always takes longer than I expect."

**You:** "How long do you spend on them?"

**Ken:** "Hard to say. I keep getting interrupted. Maybe four hours."

**You:** "That sounds about right to me."

**You:** "Would it help if you broke the job into four one-hour sessions?"

**Ken:** "Probably. But I don't know how I'd swing that."

**You:** "Block out four one-hour blocks on your schedule. Let me know when you'll be working on the reports, and I'll pass the word that you shouldn't be interrupted. Sally can take your calls."

Ken leaves the meeting with a plan. You leave with hope.

You've given them the "what" but not the "why."

Base your assignments on clear, definable goals. Tie specific tasks to those goals. Communicate those goals to the people who actually have to do the work.

**A good coach is *knowledgeable*.** Do you know what you're talking about? If you don't, employees will recognize that fact—maybe even before you do.

You'll command respect and loyalty because you know the job better than anybody else, not because you have the title and the office with the good view and the thick carpet. You'll be far more comfortable with questions when you have the answers. (When you don't have an answer, don't be afraid to say so—and then find the answer quickly.)

Knowing the job is just the half of it. You also need to know your workers—their strengths and weaknesses, likes and dislikes, work patterns and idiosyncrasies. The more you see workers as individuals, the better you'll coach them.

> ⚠ **CAUTION!**
>
> **Trust but Verify**
>
> Don't confuse "trusting" with "gullible." You'll have your share of behavior problems, personnel conflicts, and downright incompetence to deal with. (That's why you get paid the big bucks, right?) Just don't assume the negative. You should side solidly with the workers until and unless they give you compelling reason not to.
>
> When there's a problem, work with the employee to correct it. You'll wind up with a better employee—and a loyal one, too.

**A good coach is *observant*.** A few years back, Tom Peters made "management by walking around" a corporate litany. It's not good enough, Peters noted, to sit in your office, even if your "door is always open." You need to get out and mingle with the troops.

Fair enough. But wherever you are, you need to pay attention.

Being observant means more than just keeping your eyes and ears open. You need to be aware of what *isn't* said as well as what *is*, picking up on body English and tone of voice. If you're paying attention, you won't have to wait for somebody to tell you about a problem. You'll see it coming—and may be able to head it off.

**A good coach is *respectful*.** There's been a lot of talk over the last several years about achieving diversity and gender equity in the workplace. Unfortunately, there's been more talk than action, more goal setting and report writing than results. Well-meaning people disagree on the means to the end, and debate bogs down in arguments over quotas and the like. But at least the issues are on the table.

Equity requires equal access to jobs, pay, and advancement, regardless of race, ethnic group, or gender. But it goes beyond that, to a workplace where co-workers abandon limiting stereotypes and expectations and respect each other as individuals. In the ideal workplace, differences are not just tolerated—they are celebrated.

Why? Because everybody benefits from those differences. The more perspectives and personalities and values and opinions you can bring into the company mix, the more easily and naturally you can free yourself from conventional thinking and procedures.

Respect everybody around you. Respect their rights as employees and as human beings. It can be as simple as avoiding making assumptions or cutting someone a little slack, perhaps overlooking a snappish retort from a worker who's tired and stressed from a deadline you've imposed. It can be as complex as learning that a gesture you make frequently to indicate approval comes across as demeaning to someone from another culture.

A good manager tries to learn everything that might matter to the business and then applies that knowledge. Well, your employees certainly matter, so you should learn who they are and treat them all as individuals, with respect.

**A good coach is** *patient*. "How can they be so stupid?!" you wail. "I've told

---

### MISTAKE PROOFING
### Be Obviously Observant

Don't hide your talents. That's generally good advice, of course. But what we mean here is that employees should know that you're observant, that you're paying attention. When they're talking to you, maintain eye contact. You might want to take notes. Don't do anything else while they're talking. And when you're out and about the work area observing, make sure employees know you're there: nobody likes a spy.

them and told them and TOLD them!"

Patience, friend. It isn't just a virtue; it's a survival skill in the workplace. Your workers aren't stupid, and they aren't trying to drive you crazy. They're busy, and they're preoccupied, just as you are.

It could also be that they're ignorant, which is quite different from being stupid. Ignorance is curable, and you've got the medicine they need—information.

Tell them again, but find other words to do so. Using a new approach, ask them to explain the instructions to you, as if you were a new worker. That will show that they understand your directions, and it will help them internalize those directions. Remember the old saying, "To teach is to learn twice."

**A good coach is** *clear.* If they didn't hear it right, maybe it's because you didn't say it right. Maybe you just thought you did.

Everybody has seen it happen. The characters and the setting may vary widely, but the scenario is basically the same: I explain something to you, but you don't understand, so I repeat it, using essentially the same words, only LOUDER and/or more s-l-o-w-l-y. The scenario continues, with both of us getting frustrated, angry, and further apart.

Whose fault is it? Yours, for not understanding? Or mine, for failing to find a more effective way to communicate? It doesn't matter whose "fault" it is. You and I are not connecting.

Here's the bottom line: if you're trying to communicate and the other person doesn't understand, take responsibility for making the connection. Above all, don't make matters worse by just repeating the same words louder or more slowly.

**A good coach is** *assertive.* While you're being positive, enthusias-

**Assertive** Acting with confidence and persistence. Assertiveness pairs nicely with decisiveness.

Being assertive doesn't mean that you should enjoy confrontation (a trait more closely associated with being *aggressive*). Always try to work to reduce the possibility of confrontation and to minimize any potential damage.

tic, supportive, trusting, focused, goal-oriented, knowledge-able, observant, respectful, patient, and clear (whew!), never lose sight of this critical fact of business life—managers have to manage.

In other words, you're responsible for getting results. Harry Truman put it best: "The buck stops here."

Being a good coach doesn't mean you're passing on your responsibility to make decisions. It means you're making sure that you understand what's involved in any decision, that you can communicate your decisions effectively, and that your employees are willing and able to act on those decisions appropriately. That's how you get things done.

Being assertive means maintaining a strong presence. Review the preceding 11 attributes of a good coach. If you fully develop those characteristics, then you should have no trouble getting results. You can be a boss without being bossy.

### Time for a Test

Now for a quick reckoning. Take a few minutes to rate yourself on each of the 12 attributes of a good coach. For each charac-teristic, rate yourself using this scale: 5 (always), 4 (frequent-ly), 3 (50/50), 2 (rarely), or 1 (never).

| Characteristic | Rating | | | | |
|---|---|---|---|---|---|
| Positive | 5 | 4 | 3 | 2 | 1 |
| Enthusiastic | 5 | 4 | 3 | 2 | 1 |
| Supportive | 5 | 4 | 3 | 2 | 1 |
| Trusting | 5 | 4 | 3 | 2 | 1 |
| Focused | 5 | 4 | 3 | 2 | 1 |
| Goal-oriented | 5 | 4 | 3 | 2 | 1 |
| Knowledgeable | 5 | 4 | 3 | 2 | 1 |
| Observant | 5 | 4 | 3 | 2 | 1 |
| Respectful | 5 | 4 | 3 | 2 | 1 |
| Patient | 5 | 4 | 3 | 2 | 1 |
| Clear | 5 | 4 | 3 | 2 | 1 |
| Assertive | 5 | 4 | 3 | 2 | 1 |

How did you do? Obviously, 4s and of 5s speak well for you as an effective coach. But too many 5s might indicate that

### Specificity Matters

When you told Susan you needed the evaluation "as soon as possible," you understood which evaluation you meant and you knew that "as soon as possible" meant by the end of the day.

When Susan heard it, she had six evaluations sitting on her desk in various stages of completion. She didn't ask for clarification because she didn't want to look stupid and make you lose that famous temper of yours. She figured "as soon as possible" meant as soon as she got finished with the four other projects you dumped on her that morning.

When you didn't have the evaluation the next morning, you got mad at Susan. After you got done chewing her out, the feeling was mutual. Here's how to avoid the problem:

1. Think through exactly what you want done and when you want it.
2. Say so, clearly and specifically.

**You:** "Can you finish the Tyler evaluation by the end of the day?"

**Susan:** "Do you want me to do that before I finish the estimate for the Marler job?"

**You:** "I forgot about that. No. You'd better do the Marler job first."

**Susan:** "Even if I can't get to Tyler today?"

**You:** "Right."

**Susan:** "No promises, but I might be able to finish both."

**You:** "That would be fantastic. Would it help if I had Len take your calls?"

**Susan:** "Yeah, thanks."

Susan comes away with clear directions, and you have reasonable expectations. You've put Susan in a win-win position: if she gets the Marler estimate done promptly, even though it means putting the Tyler evaluation off until tomorrow, she meets the performance goal the two of you established. If she catches a prevailing wind and gets both done, she exceeds expectations.

you're dreaming. (Use this reality check: If you asked your employees to rate you anonymously, would your scores be as high?) If you gave yourself some 2s and 1s, you've identified areas where you need to do some work.

But how can you work on being more positive or observant, for example? These are characteristics, after all. You've
either got them or you don't, right?

Wrong. That's a little like saying either you're born knowing
how to do long division or you aren't. Some people take to
long division more readily than others, just as some have an
easier time mastering a language or making a balky computer
behave. But you've already learned how to do hundreds of difficult things. You can learn how to develop your coaching
attributes, too.

## How to Translate Attitudes into Actions

In the movie *As Good As It Gets,* at a crucial point in his on-
screen relationship with Helen Hunt, the waitress he is ineptly
trying to woo, the obsessive-compulsive romance novelist
played by Jack Nicholson comes up with what he hopes will
be a good enough compliment to prevent her from walking out
on him: "You make me want to be a better man."

It is, she admits, the best compliment she's ever received.
She knows she's important to him because she inspires him to
improve.

In real life, can you learn to be more patient, supportive,
clear, and assertive? Sure. You can choose your attitude—if
being a better manager matters enough to you. As with most
other tasks, you learn by doing—one trait at a time, using positive visualization and a three-week trial period.

Interested? Here's how to do it.

Pick an attribute for which you gave yourself a score of 3
or lower. For this purpose, we'll assume you picked "patient."
Develop a clear picture of what you look like and how you act
when you're being patient. You don't want an idealized picture
of how The Perfect Boss acts. See *yourself* in the role.

Mentally confront your most aggressive employee in a
highly combative situation. See yourself handling the situation
effectively and, above all, patiently.

If you're doing a good job of visualizing the confrontation,
you may feel yourself getting angry. That's normal. Take sev-

eral deep, cleansing breaths, and continue mentally working through the scenario, maintaining your focus on patience.

Replay the scene while you brush your teeth, drive to work, or wait for somebody's voicemail system to kick in. When you feel confident that you've mastered the art of being patient, put your visualization into action. The next time you find yourself in a confrontation, act as your best, most patient self.

This doesn't mean that you're repressing your true feelings. You're very much in touch with exactly how angry and exasperated you are. You just aren't acting on those feelings. Instead, you're acting with patience.

### The Boss and the Coach: A Comparison

Here's how the traits of a boss compare with those of a coach.

| The Boss | The Coach |
|---|---|
| Talks a lot | Listens a lot |
| Tells | Asks |
| Fixes | Prevents |
| Presumes | Explores |
| Seeks control | Seeks commitment |
| Orders | Challenges |
| Works on | Works with |
| Puts product first | Puts process first |
| Wants reasons | Seeks results |
| Assigns blame | Takes responsibility |
| Keeps distant | Makes contact |

In a sentence, *the coach lets the players play the game.*

### Seeing Yourself as Others See You

> **Attitude Yields Attribute**
>
> **Smart Managing**
>
> Assume the attitude, and you will develop the attribute. Sounds simple but it works.

This suggestion is for the brave only: Ask someone to hold a mirror up so you can see yourself in action.

The person who serves as your reflector must be observant, articulate, and secure enough to tell you the truth. And you have to be ready to hear that truth—and to act on it.

Explain to this person that you want her to pay attention to your interactions for the next three weeks. Describe the specific behavior you're trying to change and what you hope to accomplish. Then ask for frequent feedback.

Bringing a reflector into the process can provide two important benefits: (1) you get useful information, in the form of a description of your behavior from an outside perspective, and (2) you've increased your investment. You're a lot more likely to work on your behavior after you've told somebody what you're doing.

## The Coach's Checklist for Chapter 2

❑ Evaluate the attributes of good coaches: A coach is positive, enthusiastic, supportive, trusting, focused, goal-oriented, knowledgeable, observant, respectful, patient, clear, and assertive.

❑ Follow these steps to develop the traits of a good coach: (1) tackle one trait at a time and learn how to translate it into action, (2) give yourself a chance to make mistakes and learn from your experience, and (3) give yourself enough time to gain competence.

❑ Choose someone to be a reflector, someone who can help you see yourself as others see you. Then learn from what this person tells you to improve your coaching skills.

# What Do Your Players Want?

*I couldn't have done it without my players.*
*—Charles "Casey" Stengel*

*Can't anybody here play this game?*
*—Same manager, different players*

This book is mainly about you, the manager. But there's another side to the story, the players. You really can't get much done without them.

Charles Dillon Stengel went by the nickname "Casey." He managed the New York Yankees to unprecedented success in the 1950s, making an almost yearly habit of beating the Brooklyn Dodgers in the World Series.

He also managed the New York Mets to one of the worst won-lost records in baseball history, proving that he really couldn't get great results without good players.

But how the manager deals with the players can make a tremendous difference in terms of their performance.

Stengel invented the platoon system in baseball. Before Stengel, managers played the same eight regulars every game. The other players waited on the bench for a chance to bat for a teammate or to replace somebody in the field late in the game.

Stengel began alternating players, using a left-handed batter against a right-handed pitcher, for example, then starting a right-hander against a lefty the next day. Some players complained about being platooned instead of getting to play every day. But then, the players who'd been stuck on the bench had complained about not getting a fair chance to play, too.

Stengel wasn't trying to win popularity contests. He kept focused on the goal: to win games. And when the team was winning a lot of games and taking the World Series, the players stopped complaining. They judged Stengel by the results.

But, you might wonder, why would any of the players complain about not playing, about enjoying a good seat on the bench? After all, baseball may look like fun from the stands, but to a professional, it's a job. Players have to show up, whether they feel like it or not, and perform despite pulled muscles, headaches, and hangovers.

You and I might be able to turn off the phone and hide behind the computer monitor when we don't feel up to putting on our "game face," but athletes have to perform in front of thousands of people. They also get evaluated in public, by sports reporters and fans who can't play nearly as well, and they get booed when they make a mistake or just don't meet expectations, no matter how unrealistic.

Yeah, the game can be tough. Since players get paid whether they play or not, why don't they beg off on days when they aren't feeling their best, rather than risk poor performance or even injury?

Some do beg off, of course. But this behavior is rare—and generally held in contempt by other players. If a baseball manager puts a player's name in the lineup, that player grabs his glove and takes the field. Why?

## Looking Beyond the Paycheck for Real Motivation

Professional athletes play in pain for three fundamental reasons.

1.  The so-called salary drive explains why some athletes not only play but play their best even in meaningless games, long after pennants have been decided. They're trying to

collect impressive statistics to bring to their next contract negotiation.

2. New York Yankee great Joe DiMaggio put the second reason into words when a sportswriter asked him why he continued to play after the Yankees had clinched the pennant. "Because," DiMaggio reportedly said, "somebody might have never seen me play." He knew he was the draw, and he didn't want to disappoint anyone.

3. Most important, athletes are motivated by pride. They're the best at what they do, and they want to go out and keep doing it.

These three sources of motivation from baseball are paralleled in the business arenas. Employees want to earn tangible rewards for good performance, they don't want to disappoint others, and they're proud of what they do. The motives that stem from pride will move them more powerfully than greed or fear ever could.

## Three Drives That Motivate Your Staff

Look around you at the people with whom you work every day. From the biggest go-getter to the person who just seems to be putting in time, all are motivated by three strong forces that get them up in the morning when nothing else will:

1. the need to achieve
2. the burn to learn
3. the craving to contribute

Let's consider what each of these motivators can teach you about how to coach for peak performance in the workplace.

### The Need to Achieve

Low self-esteem has become the diagnosis of choice for poor performance these days. To cure low self-esteem, experts have prescribed praise, tons of it. That seems to be a good idea, in principle. But there's a problem: indiscriminate praise doesn't work as a reward. If everybody gets it, praise has no value. Rewards, by their very nature, must discriminate among levels of performance.

That's not to say that self-esteem isn't important to performance. The better an employee feels about himself and his abilities, the more likely he is to perform well.

So, higher self-esteem can result in better performance. But what can a coach do to promote self-esteem?

The question answers itself when we substitute a new term for "self-esteem." Let's talk, instead, about *mastery*.

> **Caution**
> Note well what we have to say about rewards here. It explains why across-the-board "merit raises" and the like are at best a contradiction and at worst a hoax. We'll take up the subject of rewards in detail in Chapter 14.

Mastery comes from what you can do, not what people say about what you can do. You *achieve* mastery; nobody can give it to you—or take it away from you.

People do things, in part, because they *can* do them. Doing them feels good. They continue to do them because they feel themselves getting even better.

Here's an example. One of the primary reasons I became a writer no doubt stems from my early mastery of typing. Seventh-grade typing class was the first place I ever distinguished myself in school. I even won the ice cream cup most Fridays for typing faster and more accurately than anybody else in class. (There was only *one* ice cream cup prize. Not only was the ice cream good; it was meaningful!)

It wasn't really the grade or even the ice cream that motivated me. And it wasn't willpower.

> **Mastery** Skill, knowledge, ability. To master a task is to be able to undertake with both competence and confidence.

(I wanted to get good grades in my other classes, too, but that didn't guarantee success.) It certainly wasn't the fear of failure and the even greater fear of looking like an idiot.

No. I typed for the joy of mastering the skill. That feeling of mastery is one of the best feelings in the world.

### The Burn to Learn

If the purpose of grading is to differentiate among students, identifying the unfit while certifying the fit for the next level, grading is doing its job.

If its purpose is to motivate learning, grading has never worked and never will. In fact, it probably does more harm than good.

Achievers learn in school to work for the external reward of the grade. In fact, many actually lose the capacity to understand whether they've performed well unless somebody tells them.

Of course, the "underachievers" are also damaged by grades. They learn to hate grades, graders, and the kids who get the good grades. And they also learn to actively resist learning anything—even by accident, even for their own good.

If sex education were taught the way English and math are taught, as more than one social commentator has suggested, the human race would die out in a generation.

Fortunately, nobody needs sex education to learn about sex. Nor, as critics of sex education suggest, does classroom instruction get students interested in sex. The interest comes from hormones, and students learn about sex through trial and error, motivated by a true burn to learn.

What's your favorite pleasure read? Some of us pick up *Sports Illustrated* or *Cosmopolitan*. Others choose a fat Danielle Steele or Stephen King novel. A few may cozy up to Dostoyevsky in the original Russian. Whatever

> **Burn to Learn**
>
> I learned to type the old-fashioned way—with a typewriter. Times change. A neighbor bought her eight-year-old daughter a typing program to run on the home PC—a game that develops manual dexterity and familiarity with the keyboard. With no teacher or textbook in sight (there's a manual, but the kid doesn't read it) and with no threat of tests or grades, before long, the kid's got the game up and running. That's the burn to learn in action.

you read, when you're reading what you love, you don't have any problem paying attention (unless you're really tired). You don't need the threat of an exam to keep turning the pages. You don't need to take notes to remember what you read. You have an inherent burn to learn.

Back when typing was the only thing I excelled at in school, I could tell you the batting averages and earned run averages of every member of the Milwaukee Braves and the Brooklyn (soon to be Los Angeles) Dodgers. If Johnny Logan went two for four, I could compute his new batting average in seconds. Yep, I had that burn to learn.

And that motivation isn't just for kids. We keep it through the years. And that's important for you to keep in mind, as a person and as a manager.

Beyond grades, beyond paychecks and performance reviews, beyond any external motivation you can create, the burn to learn makes learning inevitable.

## The Craving to Contribute

Chuck Woodbury invented the perfect job for himself and had the moxie and persistence to make it pay off. Woodbury writes, edits, and publishes *Out West*, "the newspaper that roams," a print version of the "On The Road" pieces that the late Charles Kuralt (one of Woodbury's heroes) used to do on television.

Woodbury wanders back roads, finding museums, stores, and diners, and meeting folks who qualify as "characters." Then he writes about what he sees and prints it in his newspaper. Maybe what he's doing won't change the world and maybe he'll never get rich doing it. But he's making a living and living a life he loves. His work has meaning and it gives him satisfaction.

How about you? Do you feel that your work contributes to the greater good? Long ago, many people made or grew things, real things that they could hold in their hands— machine parts or a stalk of corn. At the end of the day, they knew what they'd done and how well they'd done it. Now fewer people know that feeling of satisfaction. Some produce nothing more tangible than a computer printout. Those who still work with their hands often perform one or two simple functions, a tiny part of a much larger process, far removed from the final product.

Computer printouts are seldom a source of great pride—particularly when they're soon filed away somewhere or shredded to make way for the next set of printouts. And there's little joy, at the end of the day, in being able to say that you tightened 23,692 bolts, an increase over 23,415 the day before.

Something in us yearns to make a difference. You feel it, the farmer feels it, the cop on the beat feels that craving to contribute—and so does everybody who works with you.

If you can help employees understand the value of what they do and how it contributes to the

> **Use Statistics Wisely**
>
> Many companies, especially under the influence of Total Quality Management, have placed a greater emphasis on statistics, creating problems for managers. While statistics may help supervisors and engineers improve processes, they may not motivate employees. After all, what does it mean to the normal employee to know that production efficiency has increased by 2.4%? Far less than it means to have been an active member of the task force that brought about that increase. So use statistics to help make improvements, but remember to involve employees in their collection, interpretation, and use in making improvements.

larger picture, you'll be helping them achieve peak performance.

## Strategies for Motivational Coaching

For each of the three motivators just discussed, there's a corresponding coaching strategy you can apply.

**1. To heed the need to achieve, provide appropriate challenges.** Here are three simple tips for challenging employees:

- **Let them do the job.** Managers who don't delegate responsibility often make bad bosses. When you assign a goal for workers to reach, also assign the responsibility for achieving it and provide the means for doing it right.

- **Match the worker to the task**. Find out what each worker is good at. Plan for success rather than failure. Keep workers striving to reach the next level of achievement.
- **Focus on *process* as well as *product*.** The journey is often as important as the destination. Help employees work through the steps, gaining mastery as they go.

**2. To serve the burn to learn, create learning opportunities.** You might need to shake loose some money for a workshop, class, or conference. The continuing education department of your local college or university can provide low-cost, high-quality training. Such programs provide access to the research taking place on campus and the opportunity to get follow-up guidance later.

You can also create learning opportunities in the workplace.

**Smart Managing**

**Let them. Don't make them.** You won't have to force employees to get a job done when they work from the need to achieve. Simply create opportunities and an environment in which they can do good work.

Now, you may be thinking, "I'm not a teacher!" OK, maybe not. But often you won't need to teach; you'll just need to get out of the way. Put a challenge, the necessary resources, and workers together with a clearly defined goal and stand back. You won't teach them—but they'll learn. (We'll examine your role as trainer in Chapter 9.)

**3. To cater to the craving to contribute, give them work that matters.** Let these four simple words guide you as a coach: *"Never waste their time."*

Don't assign work just to keep somebody busy, and don't call a meeting simply for the sake of having a meeting. That behavior shows a lack of respect for your employees—and it's a waste of time for the company.

Here are two tips to help you make sure that the work you

assign has meaning for employees:

**Their actions have to count.** When you ask employees to provide input or make decisions, mean it. Otherwise, the results may be worse than if you hadn't involved them at all.

Nobody likes to commit without consequences, to work without results. It's just that simple.

If employee input doesn't really matter to you, it will show. They may not trust you again—and certainly would be foolish to ever bother trying to give you honest input.

If you tell employees to make a decision, their decision has to stick. You have to stand by it, support it, and do everything you can to make it work.

Until you're ready to make that commitment, don't set up committees and problem-solving groups. They won't do any good—and they could do a lot of damage.

### Listening Matters

I once served a term on the board of a Catholic grade school. We were under the nominal leadership of the parish pastor, but he never attended our meetings. We put in nine months developing policies regarding tuition and fees for parish and non-parish members. We struggled to be fair and felt the burden of keeping the school solvent. Our group included a CPA and a lawyer, and the discussions were stimulating and informed.

We reached consensus, drafted our proposals, and presented them to the pastor. A week later, he issued his decision—which had nothing to do with our proposals.

I really don't think he understood why some of us were upset. Since I was a volunteer, I could walk away without jeopardizing my livelihood and the well-being of my family. The people who work with you aren't so lucky.

**They need to know *why*.** I've worked with business and industry, government, higher education, and the media. As I've tried to help folks find solutions to problems and deal with adversarial situations, I've noticed a phenomenon common to employees at every level in all institutions and organizations, from the employee who scrubs the toilets to the one who signs the welcoming message on the annual report: When the going gets really tough, there's a tendency to lose track of the overall goal.

If you work at a hospital, your ultimate job is to cure the sick, to prevent the well from getting sick, and to ease the pain of those for whom you have no cure. Every meaningful task performed at that hospital in some way contributes to those goals.

Every worker in every organization needs to understand the ultimate outcome of his or her work. I'm urging you to give workers the big picture, the reason behind the work, the way their labors contribute to the cause. Because when you do, you link their work to their need to make a difference.

## The Coach's Checklist for Chapter 3

❑ Remember the three attributes that drive your employees (and you) to perform at higher and higher levels: (1) the need to achieve, (2) the burn to learn, and (3) the craving to contribute.

❑ What's the need to achieve about? Helping people gain mastery over their tasks so they feel motivated to perform well.

❑ What's the burn to learn about? People want to learn more about what they love. When they love their work, they want to learn more and get better at it.

❑ What's the craving to contribute about? People just naturally want to know how to make a contribution. When employees understand the value of what they do, they also naturally seek to improve their performance.

❑ Take actions as a coach to take advantage of the three attributes that drive employee performance to get better results.

# The Signs of
# Good Coaching

R eal coaching takes place one player at a time. Forget
those fiery "Win one for the Gipper!" locker room speech-
es (or their business equivalent, the "motivational meeting").
That's not where the coaching really happens. You'll do your
most effective coaching one-on-one, face-to-face—without
ever raising your voice.

In this chapter, we'll discuss some guidelines to help you
plan and perfect your coaching technique.

## What Your Body Language Really Says

Let's take a look at two scenarios that illustrate the positive
and the negative uses of body language to send a message.

In the first scenario, Hank hesitates at the boss's office
doorway. It has taken just about all his courage to come this
far, and now he's trying to push on for the last couple of feet.

Maureen, his boss, is frowning down at her computer keyboard, as if expecting it to tell her what to write next. She
looks up and sees Hank, and the frown deepens.

"If you're busy ...," Hank stammers.

"I'm always busy," Maureen says. "Aren't we all? But come
on in."

Her gaze lingers on the computer screen. She leans back in her chair, folds her arms across her chest, heaves a sigh, and says, "What can I do for you?"

The second scenario begins in a similar way. Hank again teeters on Maureen's doorstep, as she scowls at her computer keyboard. Sensing Hank's presence, she looks up. But this time she looks him in the eye and smiles.

"If you're busy ...," Hank stammers.

"I'm always busy," Maureen says, smiling. "Aren't we all? But come on in."

She stands, comes out from around the desk, and waves toward one of the two chairs facing each other a few feet to the side of the desk. "What can I do for you?" she says.

Same words. Different body language. And very different outcomes. In the first example, Hank will not be able to say what he needs to say, and Maureen will not hear what she needs to know.

In both versions, Maureen's words indicate that she's OK, if not totally thrilled with Hank's interruption. But in the first scene, her body language contradicts her words, sending the clear message that Hank is intruding on something important. In the second, her actions reinforce her words, expressing her willingness to give Hank time and attention.

Which speaks louder—Maureen's actions or her words?

When the two signals are at odds, employees will believe the actions every time. Hank doesn't feel welcome in the first scene and gets more nervous. He stands little chance of expressing his concerns or asking his questions. In the second

> **Smart Managing**
>
> **The Two Maureens**
>
> I'll tell you a little secret about the two "Maureens." The second Maureen, who welcomed Hank with her words and actions, was no less busy than the first one. She was no less preoccupied, under no less pressure, perhaps even no more happy to see him appear unexpectedly at her door. She just acted more approachable. You should, too, if you really want to be an effective coach.

scene, Maureen has given herself a much better chance to do some unscheduled coaching and gather important feedback.

Make no mistake—unscheduled coaching is usually the best kind, because it's more natural, having grown out of a shared context.

## The Benefits of an Open-Door Policy

There are two key reasons why you *should* welcome the employee who drops in to talk.

The first reason is that the employee gets to say what's on her mind. You want employees to feel that they can talk to you. More important, they need to know that you'll listen, that you'll pay attention to their concerns and suggestions. Lacking that assurance, they're likely to feel stifled, frustrated, and perhaps bitter and alienated. Unhappy workers don't do their best work. They'll still express their concerns, of course—to each other, when you're not around.

The second key reason for welcoming an employee is the opportunity you get to hear her concerns or questions.

You want and need to hear what each employee has to say. Gathering information about employees—about their attitudes as well as their aptitudes—is fundamental to good coaching. You can't coach them if you don't know them.

> **What Hank Knows**
>
> Hank may not be right in his perceptions of the job, his performance, other people's performances, Maureen's fairness, or anything else. Hank is an expert on only two subjects: what Hank thinks and how Hank feels.
>
> Maureen is well aware of that and may not agree with him on many issues. And she shouldn't pretend to agree when she doesn't. Nor should she promise anything she cannot or will not do or any outcome she can't or won't deliver.
>
> But she should listen and respond honestly. Every employee deserves that attention and respect.

If you *aren't* glad to see the employee who drops in to talk, fake it.

You read that right. Even if you aren't happy with the interruption, one of your options is to simply act as if you are.

Hypocritical? Not at all.

We aren't talking about how you feel. We're talking about your being a more effective manager. You need the employee's input, and that employee needs you to be willing to listen, regardless of how you feel. Acknowledge your feelings to yourself, but act on your awareness. Get up out of your chair. Work up a smile if you can. (At least ditch the scowl.) Come out from behind your desk.

Don't fake the listening, though. You must will yourself to focus on what the employee is saying. (And you'll often find that easier to do if you get up to greet the person at your door.) Remember, Hank's no dummy. He can tell if Maureen is busy, and he can usually tell if she isn't happy to be interrupted. He may even expect that, which is why he may have waited so long to come to see her and why he's so nervous about it. But he can also pick up on Maureen's willingness to put her work and worry aside, even though she doesn't feel like it. He'll appreciate her for it, because it shows him that he's important to her.

### Not Listening: They Know

If you're not really listening, employees will be able to tell. They'll sense it at the time, and they'll know for sure later when you fail to act on—or even remember—the conversation they thought they were having with you.

If that happens, you may not have to worry about being interrupted again. The employees might not be back. They don't want to waste your time, and they sure don't want to waste their own. Like Hank, they're no dummies.

With practice, you can become very convincing in the role of open, willing listener. And here's the bonus: your feelings will follow your actions. Act as if you're happy to see that employee who's interrupting your work, and you're apt to feel it, at least a little. And, once again, just the physical movements of getting up, moving around your desk, shaking hands, and so forth can really help you get out of your solo mode and into the one-on-one.

If it's really a bad time for an interruption and you can't give the employee your attention now, not even for two minutes, say so. He'll appreciate your honesty, if you handle the situation properly.

There's a good way and a bad way to do this.

If you say, "I'm busy right now. I've got to finish this report for the management meeting," the employee understands "Go away. You're not as important to me as the managers."

A better approach is to say, "I'd like to know what's on your mind, but I need to finish this report for a meeting at 10:00. How about if I come and find you as soon as the meeting ends, probably about 11:00, so we can talk when I'm less frazzled?"

> ### Now Rather Than Later
>
> Before you reschedule, ask the employee what he wants to talk about. You may find that you can address the issue in a sentence and don't need a future meeting. Ask, "What do we need to talk about?" which should sound like "How can I be prepared for our talk?" Then keep your appointment.

Here's the key: follow your "later" with a "when." If this isn't a good time, set a time that's good for both of you.

## What Really Goes On Behind Closed Doors?

"Do you mind if I close the door?"

You should.

Employees should feel that they can confide in you, ask you questions, seek your help, and bring their problems to you.

At times, it may be appropriate to hear about that problem with the door shut (as long as you realize that you've now got the attention of at least half the staff—and raised a few suspicions). But there's one case where you must keep that door open.

Joe doesn't want to talk about policies or procedures; he wants to talk about Paula. Specifically, he wants to tell you that she isn't doing her job and, as a result, he's having to carry the load for her.

**MISTAKE PROOFING**

### Keep Your Door Open

When you close your door, you may be opening a legal can of worms. Even with the door open, an employee may misunderstand something you say or do or your motives. That happens all the time, of course. But when the door is closed, when there are just the two of you, a misunderstanding may lead to greater problems.

There are numerous scenarios that could drag you out of your office and into court. Play it safe: keep your door open.

Once you realize why he's there, you need to act quickly and decisively. Don't let Joe continue to vent about Paula. Make sure you've got the gist of the complaint and then tactfully end the meeting. Tell Joe that you understand his concern, thank him for coming to you, and promise to arrange for the three of you—you, Joe, and Paula—to meet to discuss the problem.

With the three of you in the room, you've got a discussion—and both perspectives. You may well have a discussion that makes everyone involved uncomfortable, but it's a discussion. When all three parties talk, two good things happen:

- Everybody hears the same thing at the same time.
- You've got a shot at working out an accommodation that works for everyone.

## How to "Speak" Body Language

Imagine that you can't stop talking, no matter how hard you try, and you always say exactly what you feel and think. Jim Carrey made a movie based on this premise (an attorney who can't lie!) and delivered the laughs when his character got into big trouble.

In real life, it wouldn't be so funny, would it?

But consider this—your body "speaks" for you all the time, telling people how you feel and what you think through your expressions, gestures, and posture.

You show apprehension, impatience, displeasure, and disrespect with a tapping pencil and jiggling feet, with shrugs and sighs and scowls. You do, that is, unless you learn to control your body language—just as you've learned to control your tongue.

In the first scenario, Maureen folded her arms across her chest, an indicator of defensiveness. She remained seated, a sign of disrespect and unwillingness to be interrupted. She kept a huge prop—her desk—between herself and Hank, presenting a physical as well as a psychological barrier. This set up her visitor as an adversary.

In the second scenario, Maureen stood up, moved out from behind the desk barrier, and invited Hank to sit with her as an equal. (We're assuming that her chair wasn't higher or better than his. If you have two different chairs, offer your guest the better one.) Most important, Maureen made eye contact with Hank, which is the most fundamental way to create an atmosphere for an honest exchange.

By her actions as well as her words, Maureen sent a powerful message of openness and acceptance.

OK, we've got Hank in the door and sitting down. Now what?

> ### Studying Human Nature
>
> Take a moment from time to time for a nature study—human nature, of course.
>
> The next time you're in a meeting, look around the room. How are people sitting? What are their facial expressions? What gestures are they making? Then, ask yourself how those postures, expressions, and gestures make you feel. What do they say about how those people feel?
>
> You can learn a lot by taking a moment to observe the body language around you.

## The Elements of a Good Coaching Session

To conduct a good coaching session, you need to (1) establish a purpose, (2) establish ground rules, (3) keep focused, (4) avoid monologues, (5) speak clearly and simply, (6) pay attention to the issue being discussed, and (7) stay open to new ideas. Let's look more closely at each of these seven elements of a good coaching session.

### Establish a Purpose

In our example, Maureen didn't initiate the meeting; Hank did. But she needs to know the agenda, and so do you. The best way to find out is to ask.

Your tone of voice is crucial. Use a relaxed, conversational tone.

Your words matter, too, of course. If you ask, "What can I do for you?" you're assuming that you're the one who will do the helping. However, the employee may think that he can do something for you. And maybe he can. If you ask, "So, what's bothering you?" you're sending a negative message with pessimistic expectations. The employee may think that you've labeled him as a malcontent. He might feel hesitant to express what's on his mind.

Keep it simple. "What's up?" will do the job just fine.

What if you seek out the employee? The same principles apply.

---

### Don't Assume

**Smart Managing**  Don't assume the employee is there to complain. Don't assume he's there because he's angry.

And don't assume she's there because she needs something.

He says: "I want to talk about my new assignment."

You assume he means he doesn't like his assignment and ask, "What's wrong with it?"

Now both of you are on the defensive. Chances of a productive conversation are already slim.

Let's start over.

She says: "I want to talk about my new assignment."

You make no assumptions. You just say, "Sure. What about it?"

What if you don't remember what his or her new assignment is? (Hey, it happens to all of us. You really *are* busy and preoccupied, and you've got a lot of people in your department.) Don't bluff. Don't hope to figure it out while he's talking. Ask. Make sure that you're both on the same page from the start.

Although you might begin with some social amenities, keep it brief. If that employee is wondering and worrying about the reason for your visit, your attempts at being sociable are just likely to increase the curiosity and the discomfort.

Be straightforward: "I'd like to talk with you about ...."

Be respectful: "Can you take maybe 15 minutes now? Or would you prefer to set a time for us to meet?"

### Establish Ground Rules

As with any meeting, you and the employee need to have a common understanding of certain factors. The most important are time and roles.

---

### Useful Protocols

The military has a tradition of rigid hierarchies that would be quite inappropriate in a business setting. But you can still learn from military protocol.

When an officer wants soldiers to relax in his presence, he tells them so, quite clearly: "At ease." Then the soldiers know they can move about freely.

When a soldier wants to express something, she makes a request, again quite plainly: "Permission to speak freely, sir?"

Of course, the manager-employee relationship is generally much less confining than the officer-soldier relationship. But you can learn from the military that you need to maintain a professional relationship, even in a more relaxed setting or in a one-on-one meeting.

---

You need to establish a clear time frame. If the employee initiates the contact and doesn't ask you for a specific amount of time, ask how much time he needs or establish the limit yourself. ("I've got a meeting in 10 minutes. Is that going to be enough time? If not, can we meet later, maybe around 3?")

You also need to make sure that you both remember who's the manager and who's the employee. Keep things on a professional basis. Don't ask for comments "just between you and me" or the like. Don't do anything that might give the impression that whatever the employee says will be kept a secret.

If you don't maintain the manager-employee relationship in a one-on-one meeting, you'll wind up with information you can't act on and maybe information you shouldn't even have. And, of course, if you decide to act on what you learn from your conversation, you've violated the trust of that employee—and undermined the trust of any other employees who may find out about your behavior. (Quick! What's the most dangerous plant in any workplace? Yep, the grapevine.)

## Keep Focused

You'll want to keep focused on the reason for the employee's visit, of course. But there's more involved in keeping focused during the meeting. Here are a few guidelines:

- Avoid making "noise"—anything that distracts from the atmosphere. As the old song goes, "Every little movement has a meaning all its own." Whatever you do should contribute to the discussion and support your connection with the employee.
- Don't look at your computer. Not even once. Turn off the monitor. That will get rid of the temptation to look—and it conveys a clear message to the employee.
- Don't touch your papers. Again, if you might be tempted, set all papers aside on your desk as soon as you welcome your visitor. One small action can reduce the temptation and show respect and interest.
- Don't fiddle. Be aware of any nervous habits you might have and try to fight them.
- Don't answer the telephone. With secretaries, answering machines, and voicemail, the only reason to answer that call is curiosity—which suggests that an unknown caller is more important than a known employee. Always focus on your visitor.

We'll come back to this point when we talk about active listening in Chapter 6.

## Don't Give a Lecture; Have a Conversation

Don't launch into a monolog. If you're coaching effectively, your employee should probably do most of the talking.

That's true no matter which one of you initiates the session. You're the coach and the employee is the player who can benefit from your guidance. So, it's generally better for the player to act and the coach to react.

### Speak Clearly

Use words that form bridges rather than raise barriers.

Whether you're coaching an employee or meeting with other managers or whether you're talking with the man who scrubs the toilets or the woman who chairs the Board of Directors, these recommendations will help you communicate more effectively:

- Use the simplest, most common terms. Reject terms like "nonfunctional superannuated language equivalents."
- Stow the jargon. "Suicide squeeze" doesn't mean anything to someone who isn't a baseball fan.
- Be specific. Which sentence communicates more effectively, "I'm concerned because you've come to work late several times recently" or "Your on-site punctuality modality leaves something to be desired"?
- Use the known to explain the unknown. You don't have to be an English major to use metaphor and simile effectively. When you're speaking about something new and/or complex, compare it to something that's familiar to the employee.

> **Clichés Don't Work**
>
> Although comparisons can help people make connections, some of them have been abused and overused, like "level playing field" or "he dropped the ball." Avoid clichés like the plague. (Ouch!) Also, since business clichés tend to derive from sports and the military, they may cause employees who are unfamiliar with those areas to feel like outsiders. Language that seems exclusionary to an employee will only make your work as a coach more difficult.

I heard somebody on the radio describing how Einstein's theory of relativity explains the possibility of time travel. I actually understood (sort of) what he was talking about, because he compared the earth's passage through the space-time continuum to a bowling ball rolling on a rubber mat.

## Pay Attention to the Specific Issue Being Discussed

"I've got a problem with the way the office is being run," a worker challenges you. What's your response?

Let's take a moment to consider a few possibilities and the advantages and disadvantages of each response, with a little speculation about the likely results.

**Option A:** "You and me both. What's your beef?"
*Pluses*: Honest. Down-to-earth. Establishes rapport, empathy, common ground.
*Minuses:* Invites a general gripe session.
*Probable Outcome*: You both might feel a lot better for having vented, but you won't be one step closer to finding a solution.
*Hidden Danger*: You'll lose stature in your employee's eyes. It's fine that you share her sense of outrage, but you're the boss. If you've noticed a problem, why haven't you done something about it?

**Option B:** "Really? I thought things were going pretty well."
*Pluses:* Again, honest and down-to-earth. Meets the problem head on.
*Minuses:* Establishes a debate. Your worker must now "prove" herself right—which means proving you, the boss, wrong.
*Probable Outcome*: You'll shut her up. She'll appear to agree with you. But she'll walk away unconvinced and angry.
*Hidden Danger*: You won't hear from her again. And by now you should know that not hearing from your employees is your problem, not theirs.

**Option C:** "Yeah? Well, you know what they say: If you aren't part of the solution, you're part of the problem."
*Pluses:* Again, engages the issue head-on.
*Minuses:* Negative. Accusatory. Worker has to defend herself. Suggests that anyone who notices a problem better take responsibility for solving it ... or just keep quiet.

*Probable Outcome*: Worker shuts up.

*Less Likely Outcome*: Worker fights back, and you've got yourself an argument. The verbal sparring may be more productive than silence, but it probably won't get you any closer to real understanding or a solution.

*Hidden Danger*: The dangers here aren't hidden. Nobody could miss them.

**Option D:** "Hmmmmm."

*Pluses:* Doesn't lead the conversation or indicate any position. Allows the worker to set the agenda. Indicates you're paying attention.

*Minuses:* But not much attention. Psychologists get away with that kind of stuff, but it doesn't work as well for managers.

*Probable Outcome*: Your worker may have a tough time getting started without a little help. Or she may feel a need to balance your monosyllabic response by filling out the conversation, which means it's likely to take longer to get to the point.

*Hidden Danger*: You'll become known as "Mumbles" or "The Therapist."

**Option E:** "What specifically should we talk about?"

*Pluses:* You put the responsibility for the conversation where it belongs. More important, you've taken the first step toward taking the complaint from general to specific.

*Minuses:* None. You are losing control over the exchange by letting the worker take the lead, but that's a good thing.

*Probable Outcome*: The worker will tell you what's really on her mind.

*Less Likely Outcome*: The worker doesn't really have anything specific in mind and has nothing to say. In that case, you let a little silence make both of you uncomfortable. Be patient. It's OK to let her think about it. It's her move—and it's likely to be out of your office.

**Option F:** "What's the problem? Is it the way the mail gets distributed in the afternoon? I've had a lot of complaints on that. Or do you want to tell me nobody's cleaning out the refrigerator in the break room? Or maybe it's ...."

*Pluses:* You're concerned.

*Minuses:* You're giving a multiple-choice test. The worker has to choose from your menu. You may also be bringing up problems she hasn't noticed, which she may then add to her list.

*Probable Outcome:* In the best case, the worker will wait you out and tell you what's really on her mind—or try to, anyway. In the worst case, she may feel as though she's just adding to your list of problems and may assume you'll be too busy with the other problems to pay any attention to hers.

*Hidden Danger:* You thought you were communicating the fact that you're on top of things, but the employee might think you're just throwing up a smoke screen.

Pick Option E. Or maybe you've got a better option. (Just be sure to consider the pluses, minuses, probable outcome, and hidden dangers before you decide that it's better.)

---

### Three Tips for Communicating

Here are three quick tips for better communication:

**1. Narrow the focus to one issue at a time.** You'll never get a handle on the way the office is being run. But you might learn that the mail isn't getting distributed until 3:00 in the afternoon.

**2. Define the issue clearly.** No mystery here. Just make sure you're both talking about the same thing. Again, the person who brings up the issue should be responsible for defining it.

**3. Keep it in present tense.** Don't bring up the great system they had where you used to work. Stay with the here and now.

---

Whatever you do, define the issue and limit the discussion to something manageable. You'll get other chances to discuss other concerns—but only if you resolve this specific concern right now.

### Stay Open to New Ideas

If you talk about "your" idea and "her" idea, you've created two huge obstacles to finding a solution to the problem.

You've immediately limited the discussion to two possibilities, closing the door on a compromise or on a third approach.

You're talking about *you vs. her*. The struggle is personal (and one of you has to lose).

You lose either way. If you "give in" and accept the employee's solution, you may feel that you've lost some of your stature as a manager. If you refuse to give ground, if you just pound your employee into submission, you'll lose any chance of finding a better solution.

Keep the discussion open. Try to disconnect the idea from the person suggesting the idea, so you both feel free to comment, criticize, or modify. You might come up with something neither of you would have thought of alone.

And if the worker comes away thinking it was all her idea—so much the better! That boost in her self-esteem cost you nothing ... unless you're low on self-esteem yourself.

Coaching works best when it's

- one-on-one,
- goal-oriented,
- limited in scope and time,
- conversational, and
- centered on ideas, not personality.

To make your coaching sessions more productive, hone two essential conversational skills—asking effective questions and listening to the answers. We'll focus on those skills in the next two chapters.

## The Coach's Checklist for Chapter 4

❑ Make sure your body language and your words communicate the same message. If not, people will believe what your body says, not your words.

❑ Keep an open door and welcome employees when they come to talk to you—even when you don't feel like it.

❑ Here's how to set up and execute a successful coaching session: *establish a purpose, establish ground rules, keep focused, avoid monologs, speak clearly and simply, pay attention to the issue being discussed,* and *stay open.*

# How to Ask
# Good Questions

Everybody knows how to ask good questions, right? Wrong. In fact, the question you just read isn't very good, because it implies its own "right" answer, the answer you're supposed to give. It's also a trick question, because the "right" answer turns out to be wrong.

To illustrate how carefully questions must be worded to get useful information, let's take an example. Let's suppose that, as you're shopping at the mall one Saturday afternoon, you're approached by one of those smiling folks carrying a clipboard. You're about to be interviewed by an opinion pollster.

Here's the question you're asked: "Do you feel that a person who has been caught engaging in an immoral activity can be trusted to serve in high elected office?"

Your opinions about Bill Clinton, Richard Nixon, and any other public servant really aren't the issue here. But you will learn the three reasons why public opinion polls don't really tell us anything about public opinion:

**1. You'll deliver an opinion—whether you've got one or not.** Suppose you really don't care what may have gone on behind the closed doors of the Oval Office. Maybe you haven't been keeping up with the situation in Northern Ireland, either, or spending much time fretting over our balance of trade with China. But you don't want to look stupid in front of the smiling man holding the clipboard, pencil poised, waiting for your insightful comment.

So you give an answer.

Whatever answer you give, it isn't really your opinion. More likely, the pollster gets the opinion you gave because you felt you had to give an opinion. And it isn't useful information.

**2. The question means everything and thus doesn't mean anything.** In the context of the above question, what does "immoral activity" mean? It all depends on who's doing the moralizing. The term means different things to different people. Because it can mean *anything,* it really means *nothing.* How can the pollster evaluate your "Yes" or "No" without knowing your definition?

Take a look at another part of that question: "... who has been caught engaging ...." Does that mean "caught in the act"? Or does it mean "suspected" or "accused"? Maybe it means "convicted." How you interpret the wording will affect how you respond to this question.

**3. The question implies that there is a "right" answer.** Look at the question again: "Do you feel that a person who has been caught engaging in immoral activity can be trusted to serve in high elected office?"

Notice that you're being given a closed choice: your answer should be "Yes" or "No." There's no room on the pollster's chart for "Maybe" or "That depends on what you mean by 'immoral activity'" or "'Caught' in what way?" or even "Which high elected office?"

You've got to fit your answer into one of two extreme slots.

Your definition of "immoral activity," if you buy into the concept at all, probably carries a negative connotation. "Immoral" is bad. And "caught" is also bad.

On the other hand, "trusted" is good. So the wording of the question and the yes/no choice simplify a complex situation. You're being asked if you would give something good (trust) to

**Be Careful with Surveys**

People trained to construct surveys know how to minimize the dangers we're discussing here. (Whether they use caution to make their polls as objective as possible or shape the questions in order to achieve certain results is another matter entirely!)

We're assuming that you will want your questions to bring out the truth, effectively and efficiently. After all, the best manager is only as good as the information he or she uses to do the job.

a bad person (someone caught engaging in immoral activity).

You know, then, that the "right" (socially approved) answer—the one the smiling pollster with the clipboard expects from a fine, upstanding citizen such as you—is "No."

That doesn't mean you'll say "No." You might say "Yes" simply to defy social expectation. Either way, you're reacting to the way the question is worded and not necessarily its content.

## The Qualities of Effective Questions

It isn't easy to ask a question that doesn't fall into one or more of the traps we just discussed—or any others. But you'll need to ask effective questions if you really intend to get useful information from the people who work with you. That's why you need to learn the seven qualities of effective questions. Good questions are

- brief,
- clear,
- focused,
- relevant,
- constructive,
- neutral, and
- open-ended.

Let's look at each of these qualities.

**An effective question is** *brief.* So is an effective speech, marriage proposal, or court brief, and for the same basic reasons.

- Your listener's attention span is limited. (That depends a lot on interest. You probably have a little more latitude for a marriage proposal.)

- Words written on the wind tend to blow away. If your question is long, by the time you get to the end, your listener may have forgotten the first part.
- The longer the question, the more likely you are to louse it up. Short sentences aren't just easier to understand; they're also easier to say.

An effective question is *clear.* "Do you think we should veto the proposal to discontinue the policy of rejecting parts that haven't successfully gone through the non-mandatory inspection?"

That question is almost good enough to qualify as a referendum in the next election—one of those ballot initiatives that needs an explanation: "Note: A 'no' vote on this proposal indicates your support for continuing to reject parts that haven't passed inspection. A 'yes' vote means you're in favor of changing the current policy."

Now that we've cleared that up ....

If you veto a proposal to stop doing whatever it is you're already doing now, you would be agreeing to continue doing what you're doing, right? So ask, "Do you think we should keep rejecting parts if they haven't passed inspection?"

Clear questions don't use:

- *Passive voice.* A passive construction like "the offer is to be evaluated" or "the work is to be completed on time" often fails to specify something important—the person or

> ### Keeping Questions Brief
>
> To keep your question brief, think about it ahead of time. Specifically, think about two things: (1) What do you want to learn from the answer? And (2) What words will best elicit this information?
>
> If possible, rehearse, honing a key phrase or two. As you do, visualize yourself delivering the questions just the way you want to.
>
> This system works for any kind of public speaking, by the way, as well as for making more effective inquiries in writing.

people responsible for the action. So, who's going to be evaluating that offer or completing that work?

- *Fog.* Sometimes big words just happen to get in the way of communication. That's fog. (And if the confusion is intentional, as part of a smoke screen, it's called *smog.*) For example, what does the term "managerial compensatory alternatives" mean? Is it ways to make up for some deficiency? *By* managers or *to* managers? Or is it choices of payment? Again, is the payment *by* managers or *to* managers? If managers make the payment, is the choice up to them or to whomever receives the payment?

- *Multiple negatives.* We don't mean just to avoid asking questions like "Don't nobody here know nothing?" (What your fourth-grade teacher told you may be right, but it's not enough to ensure good questions.) Take our question "Do you think we should veto [negative] the proposal to discontinue [negative] the policy of rejecting [negative] parts that haven't [negative] successfully gone through the non-mandatory inspection?" No wonder it defies understanding!

**An effective question is *focused.*** Target a single subject and a particular aspect of that subject per question. If you don't, you may render any answer meaningless.

Suppose you ask, "Do you think that a simplification in the editorial process, specifically eliminating the initial discussion, the peer review, or the focus group, or any two of those steps, would result in a reduction in the quality of the final editorial product, if we also brought in an outside editor to evaluate all manuscripts before publication?"

The response is likely to be "Huh?" or "Could you repeat the question?" But even if you get an answer of "Yes" or "No," it won't be much more useful, because you won't know what it means—which you'll find out as soon as you echo that answer.

"So you think we ought to get rid of the focus groups?"

"I didn't say that. I like the focus groups."

"Well, then, you want to drop the peer review?"

"No, we need the peer review. Why would I want to drop it?"

"But you said ...."

You can imagine how the discussion goes on from here.

Break questions into their component parts, and ask them sequentially:

**Q:** "Do you think we could eliminate the initial editorial discussion without hurting the quality of the writing?"

**A:** "Sure. Those discussions are a complete waste of time."

**Q:** "How about the peer review?"

**A:** "No way. That's where we catch a lot of mistakes."

**Q:** "What do you think of the focus group?"

**A:** "It doesn't seem necessary, at least as part of the routine process."

**Q:** "What if we hired a freelancer to edit everything after we're done with it?"

**A:** "An outsider wouldn't catch the kind of mistakes I'm talking about."

**Q:** "Give me an example."

Now you're getting useful feedback, without the frustration and confusion your multi-part question would cause.

**An effective question is *relevant*.** Have you ever been "blindsided" by an irrelevant question? The surprise question might work for attack journalism "news" magazines and in television courtroom dramas, but it doesn't do much good in the office. Be clear about your purpose and honest about your motives. Keep your questions on subject and on target. If an answer strays off the point, tactfully refocus.

Suppose you ask, "What if we hired a freelancer to edit everything after we're done with it?" The response might be "First we hire a bunch of consultants to tell us how to run the production process, and now you want to bring in an editor to hack up our copy! Why don't we just can the editorial staff and ship the whole thing out?"

The mention of "consultants" sounds an alarm in your head. You were against hiring them from the start, but you got voted down. This is a perfect chance to really unload and let somebody know that the resulting mess wasn't your fault.

Don't do it. You've got another problem on the table, and

there may be no connection between the production consultants and the potential editorial freelancer.

You reply, "I share your concern about consultants, but we need to talk through the editorial process right now. I really need your feedback on this."

**An effective question is** *constructive.* You need to accentuate the positive in your approach to questioning, not because it makes you seem nicer, but because your questions will be more effective. Let's look at the difference between asking a question with a negative slant and asking a similar question in a positive way.

*Negative:* "How can we get people to stop skipping the meetings?" ["What should we do to punish people who don't come to meetings?"]

*Positive:* "How can we get people to attend the meetings?" "How can we make the meetings better, so everyone will show up?"

It's more than just a matter of phrasing. You're asking two different questions, and you'll get two different answers.

Admittedly, discussing the negative question could be a lot more fun, but discussing the positive question will be much more productive, leading to genuine improvements—which may even mean eliminating an unnecessary meeting.

> ⚠️ **Avoid Euphemisms**
> Be careful when you're taking a positive approach in order to pose a constructive question. It's easy to slip into euphemistic phrasings.
>
> *Negative:* "How can we get people to stop skipping the meetings?"
>
> *Euphemistic rephrasing (still negative):* "What negative sanctions and disincentives can we employ to ensure full attendance at meetings?"
>
> The second question will still lead to a discussion of punishments. The only difference is that you'll be using bigger words—and a lot more time—to get there.
>
> Whatever you ask, ask it clearly and simply.

**An effective question is** *neutral.* Don't confuse "neutral" with "neutered." A good question may be controversial. (The most

> ### Answer Directly
>
> Learn to avoid these common ways of using a question to direct an answer. They are generally intentional, but sometimes people just slip into them.
>
> One is the negative question. You ask, "Isn't this a good policy?" or "Shouldn't we try this new idea?" It's easy to know how to answer such questions, which means they're useless—and very likely to annoy any thinking person.
>
> Another way of directing an answer is to insert a word like "really" or "actually" into the question: "Are you really suggesting that we try that?" or "Are we actually making any progress in that project?" You're asking questions not for information but to challenge a position that you don't like, to force somebody to defend a statement or opinion. And again, you're likely to just stir up the emotional waters and muck up the dialog.

interesting ones are.) But it doesn't imply the "right" answer through biased wording.

Here's an example of the same question, first asked in a way that implies a "yes" answer, then with a built-in "no" response, and finally phrased in a "value-neutral" manner.

*Implied "yes" question:* "Do you think we should improve overall quality by hiring a freelance editor?" (Who wouldn't be in favor of improving overall quality?)

*Implied "no" question:* "Do you think we should add an extra step to the editorial process by hiring a freelance editor?" (Who would possibly favor adding an extra step?)

*Value-neutral question:* "Do you think we should hire a freelance editor?" (Well? Do you?)

**An effective question is *open-ended*.** Ask a "yes" or "no" question, and you'll get (at best) a "yes" or "no" answer. That's all. And often that's not enough.

Consider this scenario. You've got a real bottleneck in the production process. You're not sure how to unsnarl things, so you do the smart thing and ask the folks on the front line.

**Q:** "Do you think we should hire another on-line supervisor?"

**A:** "No way!"

End of discussion. If you want more, you'll have to go fishing.

**Q:** "How come?"

**A:** "It's a bad idea."

**Q:** "Do you think it would be a waste of money?"

**A:** "You bet."

**Q:** "So, you don't think there'd be any advantage to the hire?"

**A:** "Nope."

This isn't a discussion. It's pulling impacted wisdom teeth. You're no closer to an answer, or even a useful suggestion, than when you started.

If you just want to know whether the folks on the line think they need another supervisor, you asked the right question—and you got a clear answer. But if you want to explore possible solutions to a production problem, ask an open-ended question: "What can we do to improve efficiency on the line?"

But that question, while admirably open-ended, fails the "value-neutral" test, since it implies that the line is inefficient now. Instead of useful answers, you might just get defensive attitudes. Rephrase your question one more time: "What can we do to speed up production on the line?"

While not exactly value-neutral (it implies that production isn't at maximum speed), this question at least doesn't point the finger and say that production is "too slow" (a problem for which somebody must be at fault). It just says you'd like to explore ways to speed things up.

It takes a bit of thought to ask a value-neutral and open-ended question. Make sure you give it that thought.

---

**Two Questions**

Contrast these two questions for a classic illustration of the difference between a closed/biased question and an open/value-neutral one:

"Do you love me?"

"How do you feel about me?"

(By the way, an effective manager might frame the question with a positive comment about production. If you begin, for example, with "We've all been very pleased with the teamwork shown on the production line and the quality of our products," you can more easily and safely ask the question "Now, what can we do to speed up production on the line?")

## Seven Major Types of Questions

There are seven main categories of questions: factual, explanatory, justifying, leading, hypothetical, alternative, and summary. Let's take a look at when to use—and avoid—them.

**1. Factual Questions.** The question "How many on-line supervisors do we employ?" asks for a number, not an evaluation. It's a factual question.

"How many on-line supervisors do we need?" also asks for a number, but it's not a factual question. To answer, you must give an opinion.

"Is it raining?" is a factual question.

"How's the weather?" isn't factual, although it might evoke the same information: "It's raining!" It could also involve an opinion: "It's great!" (from a farmer) or "Lousy!" (from a landscaper who can't work) for the same light, misty rain.

You can verify the answer to a factual question by checking a second or third source. For the first question, count the number of on-line supervisors on the payroll (assuming they all actually carry the same job title, of course). For the second question, just stick your head outside and see if you get wet. You can never "verify" an opinion question.

> **⚠ CAUTION!**
> **Don't Argue about Opinions**
> You'll waste a lot of time if you argue about the answers to an opinion question as if it were a factual question. Since you can't verify an opinion, you can't prove it to be correct or incorrect. I can prove to you that it's raining, but I can't prove that the rain constitutes "great" or "lousy" weather.

If you want facts, ask factual questions. You may find it useful to begin coaching sessions with factual questions, in order to establish common understanding and background.

**2. Explanatory Questions.** Most kids go through a "Why?" stage. Parents of kids in the "Why?" stage often find themselves running out of answers—and patience: "Why do I have to take a nap now?" "Why do I have to eat my green beans?" "Why does Mommy wear red stuff on her lips?" "Why are those dogs doing that on the lawn?"

"Why?" is your basic explanatory question. It often makes a fine follow-up question.

"What can we do to speed things up on line?"

"Get rid of that new on-line supervisor!"

"Why?"

Be careful how you ask "Why?" Your tone of voice can make all the difference between a "Why?" that means "What makes you think so?" and a "Why?" that means "You stupid idiot."

See if you can ask "Why?" without conveying any other meaning with tone of voice, gestures, or facial expression. If you can, asking "Why?" will serve you well.

**3. Justifying Questions.** That versatile little word *why* can also function as a justifying question.

You are standing before the Pearly Gates. St. Peter looks you over, crooking an eyebrow. Is that a smirk on his saintly lips? He leans forward, pauses, and asks, "Why should I let you in?" This, friend, is the ultimate justifying question.

Asking "Why?" in response to the suggestion to get rid of the on-line supervisor can mean "Why should we get rid of the on-line supervisor?" (explanatory) or "Why do you think so?" (justifying). If you intended to ask the first question but got an answer to the second one, everybody walks away confused. Ask for what you want.

Most often, you will want explanation rather than justification. It's difficult to ask for justification without putting someone on the defensive. Too often, justifying questions sound like "Says who?" For that reason, it's best to avoid this category.

**4. Leading Questions.** As the name suggests, this type of question leads you toward the desired answer. Telephone solicitors use them all the time.

At its worst (and telephone solicitation is surely an example of the worst), the leading probe serves as a rhetorical question, which is asked to make a point or elicit a set response rather than to gather information. At its best, this type of question is still pretty annoying. Avoid asking leading questions.

**5. Hypothetical Questions.** These are your basic "What if?" questions. At their best and most useful, they call for prediction based on knowledge, an estimate, or educated guess. At their worst, they call for speculation, a "wild guess." It depends on whom you ask and why you ask them that particular question.

In either case, a hypothetical question asks a worker to comment on circumstances that haven't happened (and might never happen).

Suppose you ask the shift supervisor, "How much of a drop-off in production do you think we'd experience if we eliminated two workers from each shift?" The shift supervisor should be in a position to give you at least an educated guess, based on

> **Manipulate** To manage or control in an unfair or fraudulent way. This one comes with a warning: Don't do It. Not even once. Not by what you do, or what you say, or how you say it. Your staff won't trust you again—and they'll be right not to.

*Key Term*

past productivity and the supervisor's knowledge of work flow. But the same question, asked of one of the shift workers, probably calls for speculation.

When you ask this question of a supervisor who has already stated strong opposition to reducing the workforce, it becomes manipulative, more of a weapon than a sincere attempt to gather information.

"OK," you say, "I understand that you don't want to lay anybody off. Neither do I. But just suppose we did reduce the force by two workers per shift. How do you think we'd affect productivity?"

The supervisor grudgingly dredges up a number—which you then use to justify the layoffs. The supervisor feels manipulated—and will be wary of ever answering another question from you.

**6. Alternative Questions.** You provide the alternatives, offering a multiple-choice test. Evaluation forms provide a classic example: "Write the number that best corresponds with your reaction: 5-agree strongly, 4-agree, 3-neither agree nor disagree, 2-disagree, 1-disagree strongly."

Preference and personality tests pose an either/or choice:

"Would you rather be (a) a sanitation engineer or (b) a forest ranger?"

"Would you rather be (a) a professional athlete or (b) a college professor?"

"Would you rather be (a) Dr. Laura or (b) Dr. Ruth?"

By suggesting choices, you make it much easier to respond. But you also limit that response. Your respondent might not want to be a sanitation engineer or a forest ranger, but you've forced a choice.

The forced choice may also be manipulative. Instead of asking for a general assessment of potential layoffs on productivity, suppose you ask instead, "Do you think we should lay off one, two, or three operators per shift?" The answer "None" isn't an option.

**7. Summary Questions.** As governor of California and then as president, Ronald Reagan required staffers to prepare mini-memos on important issues. From air pollution to the Strategic Defense Initiative, Reagan wanted their best judgment rendered in one crisp paragraph.

Supporters called him The Great Communicator. Detractors dubbed him The Great Simplifier. Either way, he required that his advisors be great synthesizers.

When you ask a summary question, you're saying, "I don't have time to do the math; I just want the bottom line. I have no patience for close-ups; I want the big picture."

Summary questions often begin with phrases like "In gen-

eral" and "Overall" and can be a productive category of questions for you as a manager. Keep in mind, though, that sum
mary questions are often hard to answer and may come
across as threatening. Having to come up with an overall
assessment can take time, thought, and even in-depth research.

## Why Ask "Why?"

Asking your staff for feedback offers two immediate benefits—
regardless of the answer you get.

**When you're listening, you're learning.** No matter how useful
the answer is in practical terms, it reveals information
about the person who
gave it. You'll discover a
lot about workers' atti-
tudes as well as aptitudes
by listening to their
responses.

**When you're asking,
you're expressing respect.**
Workers may not thank
you for asking, but they'll
feel good about it. You
wouldn't have asked if
you didn't want to know.
You've brought them into
the decision-making
process and shown your
respect for their knowl-
edge and experience.

> ### Avoid "Bluff the Boss"
> **Smart Managing**
>
> Why should you never
> answer a question with a question?
> Why not?
>     If you ask a question they don't
> understand, you'd better hope they
> ask for clarification. That's a lot better
> than having them play Bluff the
> Boss—nodding, smiling, and giving
> you an answer, any answer—just to
> get you off their backs and back in
> your cubicle where you belong. Don't
> become impatient if your question
> brings a question in response. It's a
> good sign.

You win just by asking. The answer is a bonus.

## Three Suggestions for Asking Questions

Here are three suggestions on how to ask better questions and
ensure better responses.

**1. Give employees time to think.** Silence is an acceptable answer. So is "I don't know." If the question requires thought, provide time and opportunity for thought to take place. Avoid handing out new material at a meeting, for example, and then asking for an immediate response.

**2. Tell employees what's at stake.** Most of us learn to associate questions with tests and grades. The teacher knows all the answers; she just wants to see if you know them. You can be right or wrong; when you're wrong, if you're lucky, you might get partial credit.

What do employees win or lose when they answer your question? Will they be punished for a "wrong" answer, an answer you don't want to hear? If so, you'll probably never get an honest answer.

How binding are their answers? Can they change their minds later?

Will their answers make a difference in your decision? Or are you just asking to be asking?

Be honest about your motives for asking and what you intend to do with the answers. In most cases, you're asking for advice, not taking a vote. You aren't bound to act according to the advice you get. But the input should make a difference or else you shouldn't ask.

If your actions contradict the information you got, explain why.

If you ask the question simply to give the impression of wanting an answer, you'll do more damage to your working relationships than if you never asked at all.

**3. When you're done asking, shut up and listen.** We'll look at ways to become a more effective listener in the next chapter.

## The Coach's Checklist for Chapter 5

❑ Effective questions help you get useful information from the people who work with you. They also help people get at what they might not realize they know, and they help everyone realize what they need to do to improve.

❏ Good coaching questions that will help people learn and improve are *brief, clear, focused, relevant, constructive, neutral,* and *open-ended.*

❏ There are seven main categories of questions: *factual, explanatory, justifying, leading, hypothetical, alternative,* and *summary.*

❏ Here are three ways for getting better responses to your questions: (1) give employees time to think about their responses, (2) tell employees what's at stake, why you need this information, and (3) when you're done asking, be quiet and listen.

# How to Be a Good Listener

We all spend a lot of time in school learning how to communicate. We take classes in written communication and many take technical writing, business English, speech, or debate. We learn how to express ourselves.

But who learns how to listen?

It's a crucial skill for any manager, especially if you manage by coaching.

## The Seven Keys to Effective Listening

Let's explore seven basic techniques to help you be a better listener.

**1. Be prepared.** A good news reporter does background research before interviewing a source. Reporters need basic information to be able to ask the right questions and understand the answers.

The same goes for a workplace coach.

Look over the personnel file, scan the quarterly report, brush up on key terms you don't use every day. Anticipate responses and follow-up questions. As little as two or three minutes of preparation can make the difference between a useful coaching session and a mutual waste of time.

**2. Drop everything.** The biggest compliment you can ever pay another human being is your full, undivided attention. Effective listening requires nothing less. We covered this point in an earlier chapter, but it bears repeating here.

For example, don't shuffle through a stack of unopened mail, don't examine the pattern of holes in the ceiling panels or the scene out the window, and most important, don't keep working.

Time management systems teach us how to

> **Do Not Disturb**
>
> One wise manager had a very effective habit. As soon as somebody entered her office, she'd immediately reach over and hit the "Do Not Disturb" button on her phone.
>
> That move had two important effects. It kept the phone from ringing, of course. But it was also a sign of respect, offering quiet assurance that the visitor was important.

TRICKS OF THE TRADE

do two, three, even four things at once. That's great—when you're dealing with things.

For interacting with people, you should concentrate on doing one thing at a time—and doing it well. Any second activity is a distraction that risks undermining your communication—and it's likely to bother or even offend the other person. Your computer won't care if you're reading mail and checking your phone messages while running a program. But people are different. So when you listen, just listen.

Two specific interruptions (phone calls and wristwatch checking) are so intrusive that they deserve further discussion.

One of the most irritating dramas in modern daily life begins when the telephone rings. When you leap to answer it, you abandon the person who took the trouble to meet with you face-to-face. You're telling that person that somebody else is more important than he or she is. Even worse, you're actually saying that anyone is more important—since you don't even know who's calling until you answer.

Transfer your calls, so the phone doesn't even chirp. Or let your voice mail work its magic. If you don't have the technology to dodge those calls, simply meet somewhere away from any phones.

As with the telephone, so, too, with the wristwatch.

We're not suggesting you lose track of time. A clearly defined time limit is one of the hallmarks of an effective coaching session. Just stop looking at your watch when you're supposed to be listening.

If you don't think you look at that watch a lot, take it off for a day, and see how many times you catch yourself glancing at your wrist. You'll discover how watch-dependent you really are. You'll also discover that, in our society, it's just about impossible not to know what time it is, even without a watch. Time reminders are everywhere.

Here are just three ways to keep track of time without wrist-checking:

- Sit where you can see a wall or desk clock without having to turn your head. (It's a plus if you can check the time without shifting your eyes.)
- Have somebody cue you five minutes before you need to wrap up (preferably someone not involved in your meeting).
- If you have to look at a watch, do it while you're talking, not when you're listening. (That way you also might become more aware of how much you're talking, and you may listen more.)

**3. Maintain eye contact.** If you're not peeking at your watch or staring out the window, what are you looking at?

Try looking at the person you're talking with.

Lack of eye contact is one of the reasons phone conversations are more likely to create misunderstandings—even though you have tone of voice, inflection, and immediate feedback to help you. People reveal much about their feelings and comprehension through their eyes.

### Don't Lead the Witness

**TRICKS OF THE TRADE**

We're all human. We can't always control the impulse to help out in a conversation. When you're tempted to grab the words off somebody's tongue, borrow a technique from lawyers: redirect the conversation.

In court, a leading question often brings an objection from the opposing attorney. In the office, you want to be careful not to lead unnecessarily or ineffectively. But a skillfully worded and well-timed probe can save you a lot of time and frustration.

As always, tone of voice can be crucial. "Where are we going with this?" can be a gentle prod or an insulting put-down, depending on your tone—and the employee. The best probes are specific, drawing on what your employee has just said:

"Getting back to that point you made about off-site supervision ...."

"What exactly was the problem with yesterday's output?"

If you find it difficult to look someone in the eye, you probably aren't used to doing it. Take a deep breath and take a peek. Or just focus on the bridge of the person's nose, between the eyes.

But don't stare. It isn't natural to maintain eye contact for more than a few seconds. Glance away and come back. Reestablish eye contact when you want to stress what you're saying or show you're particularly attentive to what you're hearing.

**4. Hear It all before you respond.** "I know what you're going to say."

No, you don't. And saying that you do can be annoying, or worse, even insulting. It also destroys effective listening.

In your anxiety to give effective feedback—or maybe to gain control of the conversation, to speed things up a little, or even to save the other person a little effort—you may jump into a statement or question before it's finished. The result is sometimes comical, sometimes disastrous, but never helpful to communication.

> ### ⚠️ CAUTION!
> ### Put Down Your Pen
> That little pen and the simple notepad can cause trouble. We offer the following advice:
>
> Don't play with the pen and paper. It might not be distracting to move the pad around a little as you listen, but don't flip the pages or tap your pen on the desk or the pad.
>
> Don't doodle. It's a natural impulse for most people, but usually it's the graphic equivalent of twiddling your thumbs. It could suggest that you're bored or thinking of something else.
>
> Don't let your notes distract the other person. Everybody is curious about what other people are thinking, and those notes are a key to what's going through your mind. Reduce the temptation by keeping your notes close to you, perhaps even resting your hand on them when you're not writing.

Don't anticipate the end of a sentence. Don't assume you know how the statement ends, how the person feels, or where the conversation is leading.

Even if you're really good at guessing what the other person is going to say, fight that urge. Even if you're right, you're wrong for jumping in.

So, just be patient. Keep your focus. Resist the temptation to intrude. And, above all, try not to start framing answers to the next three questions you expect to get.

What if you listen to everything the employee has to say, but you still don't understand?

If you're a smart coach, you blame any communication problems on yourself, not your employee. It doesn't matter who's right and who's wrong. Your goal is to facilitate effective communication. Assume that responsibility.

Be tactful in wording your statement. Which of the following seems more appropriate: "I must have misunderstood" or "I don't think you said what you meant"?

Even if the second statement is accurate, the first is better because it expresses a result and it doesn't blame the other person for being the cause of the communication problem.

**5. Take notes.** You need to walk a fine line here. You want to

> ## Don't Write It All Down
> **CAUTION!**
>
> Don't try to write everything down. Complete
> sentences are unnecessary. Just jot down key words,
> phrases, and numbers. Leave lots of space around your jot-
> tings.
>
> Much of what you write may be useful only during the rest
> of the session. But maybe you'll need to use those notes later,
> to follow up on something or simply to keep a record of the
> conversation. If so, go over the notes as soon as possible after
> the session, filling in the blanks. (That's why it's important to
> leave a lot of space.) You'll be amazed by how much you
> remember.
>
> On the other hand, if you don't review your notes immedi-
> ately, you'll be amazed at how much you'll forget—and how
> quickly you'll forget it.

keep the discussion informal—it's a conversation, not an inquisition. So having a court stenographer sit in on your session is
a bad idea. And tape recorders of any kind are taboo, not
because of legalities (it's legal as long as you let everyone
know you're recording), but because those machines increase
the tension tremendously.

But there are several advantages to taking notes, besides
the obvious purpose of providing a record of the conversation.
Here are two benefits for you:

- It keeps you focused. Just try taking notes without listening.
- It keeps you active. As long as your hand is moving,
  you're not dozing.

Taking notes also provides benefits for the employee. It
demonstrates three things:

1. The topic matters to you.
2. The speaker matters to you.
3. You're committed to getting the information right.

If you're relaxed about taking notes, you'll be a better listener, and you'll set the other person at ease.

**6. Acknowledge feelings.** People differ vastly in the kinds and

**Get the Right Answer**

Since silence can be unsettling, some will rush to fill the void, rather than using it to think. If you feel that you've gotten a rushed, even inaccurate reply to a question, ask it again. But be careful how you do it.

"Are you sure?" may sound like a challenge. You might instead try repeating the answer, rephrasing if necessary. (Sometimes when we hear somebody else echo our words, we think about them differently.) Or you might continue the conversation, asking other questions that return to probe the point, but in different words.

amount of emotion they allow themselves to express in the workplace. Many would like to avoid feelings entirely. (We won't discuss the unhealthy effects of that tradition here.) But your conversation with a worker may go beyond fact or even opinion and into feeling.

When that happens, don't ignore the feeling. Acknowledge and verify it:

"You sound angry. Tell me about it."

"You seem pretty upset. This isn't just a distribution problem, is it?"

Our previous point about not assuming becomes especially important when feelings are involved. People carry around emotional baggage, pieces of their lives that can spill out unexpectedly. Don't assume you know what may be happening outside the workplace.

By asking, you acknowledge that the employee's feelings are important to you. You also avoid trying to deal with feelings that you only perceive, a danger that emerges in the following exchange:

"So, why are you angry?"

"Me? I'm not angry? Why do you assume I'm angry?"

"Well, I don't know. The way you stomped in here, the way you flopped down into the chair, the way you're fidgeting ...."

"Well, I wasn't angry when I came in here—but I sure am now!"

**7. Allow silence.** But don't use it as a weapon.

Silence between two human beings—especially in a tense

situation—can be intimidating. Reporters often use it as a technique to get a reluctant source to say more than he or she intends.

But a pause that allows for reflection shows respect and allows the employee to give a response that's accurate, rather than just fast.

## The Three Rs of Effective Listening

So now you know about the seven keys to effective listening. You work at following those guidelines. But how can you know if you're becoming a good listener?

To make sure you've understood what you think you've heard, use the following simple system.

**1. Receive.** To understand it, you have to hear it. Prepare. Be still. Wait. Don't assume. Take notes. Probe gently and redirect the conversation if necessary. Concentrate on the speaker to maintain your focus. Practice the art of doing one thing well.

**2. Reflect.** Think about what you're hearing. Make sense out of it. Put it into a meaningful context. Ask questions as you need to. Listening is an active process.

**3. Rephrase.** "Reflect" also means to bounce light or an image back to the source. That's the next step. Bounce what you're hearing back to the source; rephrase to make sure you're getting it right.

Do so thoughtfully, not just repeating the words verbatim or simply as a technique. Avoid psycho-speak, formulaic nonsense like "I hear you saying ...." It can be annoying and can make you focus more on the structure and less on the substance.

Don't be an echo. Put statements and questions into your own words to reflect your understanding of them.

Be open to the possibility that you've gotten it wrong. That happens: nobody's perfect. Don't get defensive. Your job here is to understand.

## Moving Beyond Listening

Effective listening is simply a means to an end. Once you're heard and understood, you must respond.

That doesn't mean you should take every suggestion, act on every criticism, or effect changes when they're suggested. What It does mean is that you must offer something in return.

If you think the employee is wrong, say so. You have the right to express your views. Just do so in the spirit of understanding, not to hammer the employee with your greater wisdom or higher authority. Share your decisions and your reasons for those decisions. If your decision is final, say so.

Employees have ideas and opinions. Don't let those thoughts disappear into a black hole in your office. (Yes, that's a cliché, but it's a good comparison here. Sometimes the gravitational force of management can absorb the brightness of employees, which then disappears without effect.)

If you don't listen and respond, employees will soon stop talking. They don't want to waste your time or their own.

Remember to talk with, not at, your workers. Practice the art of active listening, so that you can coach more effectively and make better, more informed decisions.

## The Coach's Checklist for Chapter 6

❑ Coaching means you have to listen to what employees have to say. Here are *seven keys to effective listening*: (1) be prepared to talk to the person, (2) drop everything else you're doing, (3) maintain eye contact, (4) hear it all before you respond, (5) take notes, (6) acknowledge feelings, and (7) allow for silences.

❑ Remember the three Rs of listening: Receive, Reflect, and Rephrase.

# Solving Problems by Coaching

Street law is the real law, the law that counts.
Legislators pass the laws. Courts interpret the laws. Municipalities create policies and procedures for applying and enforcing the laws. But when push comes to shove, it's the law enforcement officers who lay down the law, making split-second decisions, often with their own lives and the lives of others at stake.

That's why it's crucial that those law enforcement officers be well qualified, trained, and tested before they get out on the street.

The same holds true in your business. No matter how well you've laid out policies and procedures, street law will always be the real law.

From the hourly temp filing documents and the kid dunking a basket of fries into hot grease to middle- and upper-level managers, workers make dozens of crucial decisions every day. And they have to make them on the run.

You'll do some of your best coaching when you run with them, working out solutions and anticipating problems together.

But most often you won't be there when those critical decisions have to be made. For that reason, you need a well-coached team of workers, capable of making decisions, taking

### The Less Control the Better

"My people won't make a move without me," Paul brags to anyone who'll listen. "I make sure they check everything with me first." He laughs. "In fact, they're flat out afraid not to!"

Instead of bragging, Paul ought to be looking for another job. He's not doing his job as a manager. He's too busy trying to do everybody else's job.

Maybe you'd like to think that the whole works would fall apart if you weren't there to run everything, but you can't afford such self-indulgence. Trying to make yourself indispensable is just plain bad management.

Coach workers so well that they're confident to make decisions without you and capable of making good ones.

The better the manager, the less control he or she needs over workers.

initiative, and solving problems.

How do you put together such a team?

- Hire them carefully.
- Coach them well.
- Give them room to work.

You want to avoid having to spend your time checking and correcting workers. Put in that time up front, coaching workers to do the job right the first time, without you looking over their shoulders.

If you coach them well, you won't have to correct them later.

## Seven Steps to Effective Problem Solving

In problem-solving sessions, effective managers follow these seven steps:

1. Define the opportunity.
2. Define the goal.
3. Create the action statement.
4. Create the action plan.

5. Set the evaluation standard.
6. Confirm understanding.
7. Plan the follow-up.

Let's take those seven steps one by one, from the top.

**Step 1. Define the opportunity.** Although it may seem like part of a hokey management mantra—a problem is a challenge, a challenge is an opportunity, an opportunity is a triumph. (Defining the opportunity really does help you create solutions if you look at any situation as a challenge or an opportunity rather than as a crisis or a problem.)

Whatever you call it, you and your staff need to know exactly what it is you're all working on.

Sometimes that means you, as the coach, need to do a lot of asking and a lot of listening. "Why?" and "How?" questions are your best tools here.

You may go into a coaching session believing that the problem is Frank's rotten attitude and lack of motivation. By the time you're done asking and listening, you've redefined the problem as a lack of meaningful work for Frank to do. So, it's an opportunity to put Frank where he can contribute more value to the company and find greater job satisfaction.

Make sure everybody involved has a clear and consistent sense of the opportunity before you move on to step 2. If anyone still sees it as a problem, you may need to devote more time and creative thinking to step 1.

**Step 2. Define the goal.** Once you get the opportunity mapped out, the goal usually seems obvious. But that's often only in appearance. Let's take an example.

You're not selling enough harpsichords? Then sell more harpsichords, right? Of course. But to whom, and for what purpose?

Do you go back to your old customers, trying to persuade them to buy more? If so, for what reason? Do you have a new use for your product? ("The harpsichord—your musical salami slicer.") How about a new occasion to use it in the same old way? ("The harpsichord: it's not just for after dinner anymore.")

Do you try to open up a new market? If so, how will you identify and reach those people? Why aren't they buying from you already?

"We need to sell more harpsichords" isn't a clear enough goal.

Let's try, "We need to develop a market for harpsichords among the nearly 200,000 owners of Harley-Davidson motorcycles in our marketing area." That's a clear goal. (It may be nuts, but it sure is clear.)

**Step 3. Create the action statement.** How are you going to market those harpsichords to Harley owners? You need an action statement.

The action statement simply recasts the definition of the goal and explains how that goal will be achieved: "We will develop a market for harpsichords among the nearly 200,000 owners of Harley-Davidson motorcycles in our marketing area by personally visiting every one of those owners in their own homes and giving a demonstration recital."

**Step 4. Create the action plan.** Get out the map, carve up the districts, develop deadlines, and send the troops out into battle.

Don't adjourn the meeting until you've got a specific plan—if not the entire process, at least the first step. Everyone should leave with a clear idea of what they're supposed to do next and how soon they're supposed to do it.

**Step 5. Set the evaluation standard.** How will you know if the action plan is working?

It's amazing how often people launch action plans without considering that basic question.

If the goal is simply a canvass of every Harley-Davidson owner, then a chart, a timeline, and a felt marking pen are all the evaluation tools you need. When you've checked every name off the chart, you're finished.

If you expect something to happen as a result of your canvass, evaluation becomes a bit trickier. Define the desired result qualitatively and quantitatively. What do you want the

Harley-Davidson owners to do? (Send for more information? Sign up for a free trial lesson? Give you a down payment?) How many of them do you need to get to do it for the project to be considered a success? (If the harpsichords are priced at $500,000 each, you may need to sell only one to have a successful cam-paign.)

**Step 6. Confirm under-standing.** Before you end the session, make sure that everyone has the same clear understanding of what you've decided.

**Step 7. Plan the follow-up.** Make sure everyone has specific marching orders and a time for the next session, if any. Don't leave it open-ended. The follow-up plan might look like this:

> **Ensure Mutual Understanding**
>
> Here are five ways to ensure mutual understanding of the plan:
> 1. Get everyone involved in the for-mulation.
> 2. Repeat key points.
> 3. Paraphrase those key points.
> 4. Seek feedback at each step.
> 5. Put it in writing.

- Dave types up the draft memo and gets it out by e-mail to the rest of the group by tomorrow morning.
- Every unit manager gets his or her input on the draft back to Dave by noon.
- Dave sends out a final draft by 3:00.
- Managers circulate the memo to members of their divisions and get as much feedback as possible.
- The group meets again in one week (same time, same place) to compare responses and draft the final report.

## Dealing with Degrees of Difficulty

We just presented a formal process for creating solutions through coaching. We stressed up-front planning and discussion, with clear communication and feedback to remove mis-understandings, before the job begins.

Some coaching sessions are much less formal, of course, but they still follow the same basic pattern.

### Low Degree of Difficulty: The Case of the Clogged Commode

"Hey, boss! The toilet's backed up in the men's bathroom."

"Well, let's unplug it."

"You want me to call a plumber?"

"No. We can handle this. There's a plunger in the utility closet off the entryway. If that doesn't work, we've got a snake in the basement."

"By 'we,' you'd be meaning 'me'?"

"Yeah."

"OK. I'll get to it right after I finish the ...."

"You'd better do this first."

"Yeah. I guess you're right."

"Check back with me when you're done. If you have any problems, give a holler."

"Right."

Believe it or not, even this simple exchange follows the seven-step process. Take another look. They're all there (more or less).

1. Define the opportunity.

"The toilet's backing up in the men's bathroom."

2. Define the goal.

Implied. Unplug the toilet.

3. Create the action statement.

"You want me to call a plumber?"

"No. We can handle this. There's a plunger in the utility closet off the entryway. If that doesn't work, we've got a snake in the basement."

4. Create the action plan.

"By 'we,' you'd be meaning 'me'?"

5. Set the evaluation standard.

Again implied. When the toilet flushes freely, you've reached the goal.

6. Confirm understanding. "OK. I'll get to it right after I finish the ...."

6a. Clarify confirmation. "You'd better do this first."

6b. Reconfirmation. "Yeah. I guess you're right."

7. Plan the follow-up. "Check back with me when you're

done. If you have any problems, give a holler."

"Right."

Nothing to it, right? At least at this low level of difficulty....

### Medium Degree of Difficulty: The Problem of the Personnel Pig Sty

**1. Define the opportunity.** You've gotten a lot of complaints about the break room. Folks are leaving dirty coffee mugs in the sink, nobody's cleaning the coffee filter, and the pot hasn't been washed since the invention of decaf. There are little live things trying to seep out of the refrigerator. The door of the microwave has crusted shut.

**2. Define the goal.** At your monthly department meeting, you quickly reach consensus on the goal—get the place cleaned up before you have to hire a bulldozer and level it.

**3. Create the action statement.** Agreement is a lot harder at this stage. In fact, discussion gets rather heated. Some potential solutions are presented:

"Naming no names, but the whole mess is being generated by just a few. I say we make them clean it up!" [That suggestion generates a rather strenuous discussion.]

"I say leave it as it is. If people want to wallow in a pig sty, let 'em." [This suggestion is greeted by a chorus of "Right on!"]

"Circulate a memo outlining a policy on cleanliness, with clear penalties for non-compliance." [This is met with loud, widespread groans and scattered hooting.]

"Hire a cleaning service." [General cheers.]

"Shut it down. If people can't behave properly, they don't deserve the privilege of a break room." [The person making the suggestion is invited to swig poison.]

"Make the brass use the same room as the rest of us. They'd make sure it got cleaned up soon enough." [Laughter.]

"Why not just rotate the duty? Have a sign-up list for making the coffee and cleaning the pot. Everybody washes their own mugs. We clean our stuff out of the refrigerator on the last Friday of the month. Last one out unplugs. We rotate who cleans it out the following Monday." [Silence. A few nods. "Yeah. That makes sense," someone mutters. An action statement is born.]

**3a. Refine the action statement.** When someone says, "I never use the room. Why should I have to clean it?" you respond, "Good point. We'll limit the sign up to the people who use the room."

**4. Create the action plan.** Here's where a good, simple plan can fall apart. Everyone agrees. With the best of intentions, they leave the meeting, confident that "we'll get that break room cleaned up now." Then nobody does anything.

In the absence of volunteers (a common situation, unfortunately), you'll have to assume the leadership role, appointing someone to make the sign-up list and get things going. (Try to resist the natural temptation to automatically stick the person who came up with the suggestion. You want to encourage innovation, remember?)

**5. Set the evaluation standard.** Does somebody have to be "in charge"? That's a tough question. Human nature being what it is, if everybody is equally responsible, then nobody's really responsible. But avoid setting anybody up as a "cleanliness cop"—especially you. Let the users set the standards; if it's good enough for the folks who take their breaks there, it's good enough. Nobody said anything about bringing in placemats and cloth napkins.

**6. Confirm understanding.** "OK, Frank. You're going to post the sign-up list and take coffee duty for the first week, right? And we'll all get our stuff out of the fridge by Friday afternoon. I'll take first crack at mucking the thing out Monday."

**7. Plan the follow-up.** "Let's give it a month to see how it works out. At our next meeting, we'll decide if it's working."

### High Degree of Difficulty: The Pencil Puzzler

A play in one act with two roles—The Coach (you) and The Assistant (Connie).

You've got half a ware-house full of #2 Ticon-deroga pencils.

"Guess I overordered," Connie says.

You mentally note that she doesn't make excuses or try to pass the buck.

"Guess you did," you acknowledge, "or else we undersold. Either way, we've got an opportunity on our hands."

Connie grins. She's used to you using words like "opportunity" when

### Don't Forget to "Do It!"

There's a very important eighth step we haven't talked about yet. After "Plan the follow-up" must come "Do it!"

You've got to follow through on the follow-up. If necessary, use Post-It reminders, calendar notations, and computer tickler messages to remind you of what you promised to do and when you said you'd do it.

If you don't follow through on the follow-up this time, nobody's going to play along next time.

you really mean "monumental screw-up," but it still makes her smile.

"What should we do?" she asks.

You fend off the initial flood of anxiety that comes naturally to all of us who have been trained to believe in the Doctrine of Management Infallibility. It's taken a while, but you've learned better. The boss doesn't always have the answer. But the coach can help to create one.

"Let's talk about it," you suggest. "What do you think we should do?"

Connie's used to this approach, too. She's not scared or defensive, thinking you're just turning the gun back on her. She knows you intend to help her.

In the next five minutes of discussion, you quickly decide on the goal—to get rid of all those #2 Ticonderoga pencils—and a secondary goal—to avoid making the company look foolish for ordering too many pencils.

But getting to the action statement takes a little longer. Your discussion generates these possibilities, among others:

- Get loyal pencil buyers to use their pencils more often by creating a back-to-basics, technophobic campaign. Henry

David Thoreau (the son of a pencil maker, by the way) will serve as your patron saint.

- Soak the erasers in some mild corrosive so that they will wear out after only a few serious rubs—thus rendering the pencil virtually useless.
- Slash the price of pencils drastically.
- Taking a page from the baking soda people, create new uses for the pencil as kindling, tent poles for the Flea Circus Big Top, earring backs (just the eraser part—duh), back scratchers, gardener's helper (punch the hole for the seed, mark the row, aerate the soil), and cat toys (check out what they're selling for cat toys—and the prices they're getting!).
- Burn the warehouse and claim the insurance.

MISTAKE PROOFING

### Make Brainstorming Work

When you're brainstorming for solutions,

- Don't discuss the merits of any solution until you're sure you've created as many possibilities as you can. The focus should be on creativity, not critical analysis, and on providing quantity, not ensuring quality.
- Separate the idea from the person who proposed it. You want to discuss possibilities, not personalities. Let others build on and modify any ideas proposed. Not only does this approach lead to better ideas, but it also encourages the whole group to assume ownership of them. And that makes it easier to implement whatever ideas seem best.
- Ruining the erasers is clearly a hare-brained idea, slashing prices may not be feasible (the profit margin on pencils being rather slender), and you wouldn't really become a party to insurance fraud. But you should note each idea and go on to another.

By the way, it's OK to laugh—if the idea is intended to be funny. It may even be a good idea. However, never laugh at serious suggestions. Nothing can kill a creative mood faster than ridicule.

You settle on a solution. You'll launch a celebrity testimonial campaign, using Chuck Jones as your spokesperson. (Chuck Jones invented the Roadrunner vs. Coyote classics and gave Bugs Bunny his personality.) As fate would have it, Chuck Jones, creative superstar, uses the #2 Ticonderoga pencil exclusively.

Your slogan: "Be like Chuck!"

Once you've decided on your solution, it's downhill sledding as you frame your action plan and means of evaluation, confirm your understanding, and schedule the follow-up.

> ### Don't Rush Your Decisions
>
> You might not have to make a decision immediately, and it might be a good idea if you don't rush it.
>
> The bigger the opportunity, and the more that's at stake, the more likely it is that you'll want to defer a decision until a second coaching session. That gives everyone time to seek feedback and more ideas, of course. It also gives the subconscious mind a chance to mull things over— and possibly give you one of those wonderful middle-of-the-night "Ah-ha!" revelations.

The more you use this technique of problem solving through coaching, the more you're likely to find that the solution isn't really the major challenge. You're apt to encounter the highest hurdles when you try to define the opportunity.

Let's look at another example.

Sales personnel at your retail outlets don't seem to be sensitive to fluctuations in the pricing structure. (Translation: they aren't changing the prices when you tell them to.) That's what doctors would call the "presenting symptom," like a bad rash or a persistent cough.

But what's really the problem? There are three possibilities:
1. You've got idiots for salespeople. If so, you should have other evidence of the idiocy.
2. They've got some reason for defying the "edict from on high." That possibility might be worth talking about.
3. They aren't getting the word when you think they are.

Put your money on the third possibility—though you might

> ## Get Them Working with You
> As in *Animal Farm,* all people in the company are equal, but you as manager are of course more equal than Connie. Yet, as an enlightened coach, you know it's a lot more productive to encourage Connie to work *with* you rather than *for* you.
>
> You and Connie created the solution together. If the "Be like Chuck!" campaign succeeds, you'll share in the glory. In fact, as a wise coach, you'll step aside and let your player have the spotlight. (After all, the better she looks, the better you look.) If the idea flops, don't let Connie take the fall. Now's the time for you to step forward and shoulder the responsibility.
>
> You haven't given that responsibility away by coaching. You couldn't, even if you wanted to. It's still your call. You just reached your decision in a better way—better because collaboration helps employees develop, and better because you had more input before you made it.

need to do a bit of investigation before you move on to the action stages.

You're currently getting the word out on prices through a confidential bulletin, which goes out via first class mail the last Thursday of every month. The salespeople should be getting the letters on the following Monday, which would give them a week to implement changes before your deadline of the seventh of the next month.

In case the bulletins are getting lost or delayed in the mail, you start faxing them—and nothing improves. (Everybody blames the post office for a variety of failures, but that system is actually amazingly reliable. The hold-up is usually closer to home.)

A little sleuthing reveals that the salespeople aren't reading your bulletin. (It has, in fact, become the ultimate "confidential" bulletin: nobody knows what's in it.) Many of them weren't even aware that they were receiving it.

Now you're ready to brainstorm solutions. You might pursue "ways to get them to read the bulletin." (Redesign. Bribery.

Pop quizzes tied to salary adjustments.) But by limiting your-self to that focus, you ignore the broader question: Is a bulletin the best way to communicate this information? How else might you do it? Ask the people involved.

Asking the right peo-ple the right question is the essence of good coaching. You'll get your players involved in the process, you'll get a bet-ter answer, and they'll all own that answer when it

> **Create the Solution**
>
> You're not looking for the "right answer." You're creat-ing a solution you will all act on together.
>
> Seeking the "right answer" will prevent you from being able to settle on any solution.
>
> **Smart Managing**

comes time to put it into practice. And that generally means less effort.

Structure problem-solving sessions so that everyone par-ticipates in creating the solution, and everyone is clear about who does what to make it work.

Problem solving may well be your most important—and most challenging and stimulating—role as coach. But you have other crucial functions, which we'll discuss in the next three chapters.

## The Coach's Checklist for Chapter 7

❑ An important goal of a good coach is to help people learn how to solve problems on their own. To do that, you should hire them carefully, coach them well, and then give them room to work.

❑ Here's an effective seven-step methodology for coaching employees to solve problems: (1) define the opportunity (problems are always opportunities in disguise), (2) define the goal, (3) create the action statement, (4) create the action plan, (5) set the evaluation standard, (6) confirm the understanding, and (7) plan the follow-up.

❑ Understand, as a coach, how to apply this methodology to problems of different levels of complexity.

# The Coach
# as Trainer

et's start with three images.

Years ago, Clyde Beatty was the most famous lion tamer in the world. Confronting those wild cats, a chair in one hand and a whip in the other, Beatty would thrust and lunge, the lions would roar and claw, and then Beatty would get those huge hunks of ferocity to sit up on chairs, roll over, and otherwise shame their heritage.

A frequent scene from the old Westerns that used to be shown at Saturday matinees has cowpokes sitting on the corral railing, watching one veteran bronc buster after another get thrown by a raging mustang.

"Nobody can break and gentle old Fury," one grizzled vet asserts.

"Bet I could," says the fuzzy-cheeked new kid.

The camera cuts to the kid, clinging to the infuriated horse that's whirling, bucking, trying to scrape the kid off on the railing, all but jumping out of its hide in its efforts to throw its rider.

The kid, of course, breaks and gentles old Fury, earning the grudging respect of the rest of the cowboys.

Let's look at another image. The grizzled drill instructor

confronts a new crop of recruits. Disgust floods his face as he walks up and down the line of ragtag misfits, which he must, of course, shape into an efficient fighting machine by the second reel.

Most of the recruits look scared. One wears a smirk.

"Something funny?" the DI asks, getting in the recruit's face.

"No," the cocky kid replies, adding "Sir" a beat too late.

The DI rides the kid mercilessly, singling him out for physical punishment and verbal abuse.

The kid takes everything the DI can dish out and, in the process, learns to become *a man*.

Why begin this chapter on the coach as trainer with these three images? Only to reject them as examples of training. When we talk about your role as a trainer, we don't mean lion taming, bronc busting, or molding raw recruits into Marines.

Don't confront the trainee with a whip and a chair. Don't get on the trainee's back. Don't get in the trainee's face.

One more image, common to us all: the teacher holding forth behind the lectern at the front of the classroom, carried away by the sound of his or her own voice, while all the students slumber. Nope. That's not the picture we want, either.

Come out from behind the podium. Stand shoulder to shoulder with the learner. Only then will you be ready to teach and train—and learn.

## Guidelines for the Coach as Trainer

If you can't do it, you can't teach it, either.

The first requirement to be an effective trainer is mastery of the task. It's fairly common today for top management to bring in a supervisor from another area to take over an operation. Some supervisors receive only management training and join an organization without being familiar with the products, services, or processes involved.

If you find yourself in this position, your first job is to learn before you teach. Take every training opportunity that presents itself and that you can seek out, including informal on-

### It's OK Not to Know

Maybe you've heard this advice: Don't ever let on that you don't know. Nonsense.

Too many managers try to hide their massive ignorance behind their slender knowledge. It's like trying to hide an elephant behind a palm tree.

Employees figure out soon enough that you don't know what you're doing (or not as much as they do). You're a lot better off letting them know that you know it—and that you're willing to learn. Don't be afraid to ask "ignorant" questions. The only truly ignorant question is the one you won't let yourself ask because you're worried about looking bad.

Be open about your ignorance. Just don't remain in it.

the-job training. Read. Observe. Ask questions. Do your homework. Don't be too proud to ask those who work "for" you to become your teachers.

Simply knowing the job isn't enough to enable you to teach it effectively. Just watch somebody who has been driving the same route to work for 25 years try to give directions to a new hire who has just moved into the neighborhood.

The first guideline for good teaching, then, involves what you do before you start.

### Prepare to Present

Think through the process you're going to teach. Break it down into steps. Keep things as simple and direct as you can, but be careful not to skip steps. If you've done the job for a long time, you may not even think about some of the steps involved. Approach it from the point of view of someone new to the task, the machinery, or the process.

Use simple, direct language. If workers will

### The 3 x 5 Card Trick

Jot key steps in a process on a 3 x 5 card. If the process won't fit on one side of a 3 x 5 card, simplify your explanation or divide the process into simpler subprocesses. When trainees master the subprocesses, they've also mastered the whole process.

need to know technical terms, use and explain those terms. If they don't need them, don't even bring them up. Give them what they need, no more, no less—not what you want to teach.

Rehearse. No matter how well you know the process, you need to practice explaining it. Go over the steps in your mind several times—first thing when you wake up, on your way to work, and again a few minutes before you start the training.

Practice key words and phrases you'll need to use.

> ### Don't Memorize, Prepare
>
> Don't write out your presentation word for word, and don't try to memorize specific language. You'll be as animated and friendly as the zombies in *The Night of the Living Dead*, and questions and comments will catch you off guard.
>
> Prepare thoroughly enough to look like you're winging it. That's the key to effective presentation.

Anticipate questions and practice answers. (If you get a question you can't handle, admit that you don't have an answer and make it your business to get one (as soon as possible).

Even five minutes of this kind of rehearsal will pay real dividends in terms of your ability to communicate clearly and to get your trainees up and running at the level you expect.

## Prepare to Demonstrate

You've got it all over a training manual or demonstration tape. You can get feedback, verbal and nonverbal, and you can answer questions. You can watch workers try things and see how well they understand. Most important, you can put your hands on the equipment and show while you tell.

Work through the demonstration at least once and preferably a few times before you attempt it for trainees. If possible, work on the same equipment you'll use for the demonstration.

## Apply the KYHO Principle

After you've demonstrated the process and answered questions, step aside and let them do it. Resist the temptation to do

> **⚠ CAUTION!**
>
> ⚠ ⚠ **Enable Them**
> They haven't learned it until they can do it without you.
>
> Your job as trainer isn't to teach employees. It isn't even to get them to learn. Your job is to enable them to do it.
>
> It's all in the application. All your childhood, you watched somebody else drive a car. Then the motor vehicle department gave you a manual to study. That wasn't enough. You learned how to drive with someone beside you. That still wasn't enough. When you actually became able to drive by yourself, that was what really mattered.

it for them the first time they falter. Stick to the Keep Your Hands Off principle. Answer questions. Give prompts. But keep your hands clasped behind your back.

Never show off your mastery. The teacher isn't the star here—even though you might have the spotlight on you for awhile. The learner is the focus.

If the demonstration doesn't work, take a few deep breaths, think through the process, and try it again. Let your trainees in on the fun. "OK, guys. What am I doing wrong here?" Don't try to fake it. Say, "I just did that to see if you were paying attention" only if that's really the case.

### Train for Small Successes

Teach enough but not too much.

Don't parcel out information in such small doses that they must keep coming back to you for each new step. ("OK, as soon as you've practiced booting up for a while, I'll come back and show you how to get into the word-processing program.") This fosters dependence, slows the learning, and frustrates learners. Give them enough to let them to carry out a process without your being there. Let them get into the process quickly enough to experience and appreciate it.

It's the difference between making beginning guitar students practice three chords over and over for weeks and teaching them to play a simple three-chord song. The first approach is boring and frustrating. The second is fun (which is why they call it "playing," not "working," the guitar).

But don't load on so much all at once that they're bound to fail. Progress at the pace of the learner. If you're training more than one person, and they're progressing at different rates, separate them if you can, so the faster learner doesn't rush the slower one past important steps, and the slower one doesn't frustrate the speedy learner.

Offer praise and reinforcement if appropriate and if you're comfortable doing it. Try to keep criticism to a minimum. Don't say anything that doesn't seem honest and natural to you. And remember, what you say isn't as important as what you let them do.

> ### Let Them Figure It Out
> **Smart Managing**
>
> When employees stumble at a task, again resist the temptation to do it for them or even to tell them immediately what they did wrong and what they should do. Instead, employ the coach's greatest tool—the question. "What do you think went wrong there?" is much more effective than "Here, let me show you again." The first approach communicates your confidence in them and keeps the learner actively involved. The second takes the task out of the learner's hands.

### Foster Mastery and Independence

Never lose sight of your true goal as a trainer—to put yourself out of a job as soon as possible.

If they walk away from the training session convinced they did it all themselves, fine. You aren't in this to get credit. You're in it to coach workers to peak performance, including acquisition of new skills and techniques.

Smile if you hear them say, "Ah, there's nothing to it. I probably could have picked it up faster without any help." They're really saying that you did your job well.

## Before, During, and After Training

New hires come in with experience, certificates, and degrees attesting to their competence. But somehow they don't seem to know what you thought they would.

They, like you, are victims of a changing work world where what we learned yesterday is no longer very helpful today. Your systems may not look anything like what the new hire worked with just a few months ago in school or at his or her previous job. And that newcomer returning to the workplace after a time out for other pursuits may be several generations behind. Therefore, make sure that you take the time necessary to address the issues specific to each stage of the process before moving on to the next phase.

### Before You Start Training

Explain clearly what the learners are going to do and why they're going to do it. Describe the specific goals. Define the desired outcomes.

If you just dive right in, you're much more likely to encounter snags and frustrations. It's harder to do something right if you have to undo something wrong.

Take the time here. It will save you time later.

### While You Train

Take it one step at a time, demonstrating, observing, commenting. Get feedback from the workers at each step. It's a lot easier and less frustrating to keep them on track than to have to figure out where they are and get them back on track later.

### After You Train

Be ready with feedback, and stay open to questions.

Don't assume that, because you walked them through it once, they've got it forever. Some people can learn quickly, while others need to go through the process many times.

### Two's Company, Three's a Crowd?

The best training often takes place one-on-one, which helps explain why the most effective training occurs spontaneously on the job. It also explains why you, and not a hired outside trainer, will wind up doing a lot of the teaching.

However, in some situations, one-on-one training isn't effective, because there's too much attention on the individual learner, who becomes overly self-conscious. And that extra attention may not even be necessary, especially if the task requires a lot of practice and not much supervision. Sometimes you'll need to teach employees in groups, not only to save time, but because they'll pick it up faster that way.

## What Kind of Trainer Should You Be?

You've probably had gruff teachers and jovial teachers, distant teachers and teachers who wanted to be your pal, strict teachers and hang-loose teachers. What kind should you be?

You should be *yourself*. Of course, that means you should want to be your best self—prepared, focused, attentive. But it also means that you should train in a way that comes naturally to you. There are really only two basic qualities you must have to be a good trainer:
- You have to know what you're teaching.
- You have to genuinely care about your students.

No matter how well you've seen a technique work when somebody else used it, if it feels phony to you when you try it, don't do it.

## Effective Training—From the Learner's Point of View

Let's invite your students to tell you what they need from you as you train them in the workplace. Follow these nine simple principles, and everyone will get the most out of every training session.

**1. Remove the distractions.** I'll give you my attention while you teach me, but you've got to do your part by eliminating anything that will get in the way.

Potential distractions include
- your telephone, beeper, and pager;
- my telephone, beeper, and pager;
- "buzz" (irrelevant noise);
- "flicker" (irrelevant visual stimulus); and
- an audience.

**⚠ CAUTION!**

### Don't Sell Tickets

You may want to involve several learners in the process at the same time. But you don't want to let others stand around and watch while someone else learns. Learners as spectators can pass judgment and inhibit learning—even if they don't say or do anything.

But if everyone is involved, taking his or her turn trying the process, all the learners are in it together, sharing the frustrations and anxieties of learning. Also, they may tend to help each other—maybe in ways that you couldn't imagine—which facilitates learning and builds team spirit.

**2. Respect my intelligence.** I'm your learner. You're my coach. You know what I need to know and how you want me to do it. But that doesn't make you smarter than me.

I may be ignorant about this process, but I'm not stupid. There's a big difference. Ignorance is a temporary condition. I can learn—if you'll help me and let me.

Don't talk down to me. Don't lecture me. Don't disrespect me. If you do, I can guarantee that you won't teach me anything. I won't let you.

**3. Respect my time.** I know you're busy. You've got all that important manager stuff to do. But I'm busy, too. I've got worker stuff to do, and my stuff is just as important to me as your stuff is to you.

I've also got a life outside the workplace, just as you do. I want to have time to live and enjoy that life.

I don't resent good training. I need it, and I want to learn. But I do resent unnecessary training, interruptions during the training, and repetition after I've already got it. Don't make me run laps just to keep me busy, coach. Let me get it and get on with it.

**4. Take one step at a time.** You can do this stuff in your sleep. But to me it's new. So give me the big picture, what it's supposed to look like when it's done, but then let me take it one step at a time.

**5. Take small enough steps.** Your definition of a "step" might not be the same as mine. Match your pace to mine in the

### Learning Is Natural

Just why *can't* Johnny read?

After all, he learned to talk, and that's surely one of the most amazing feats of learning imaginable—and he did it before he knew what learning was.

He listened, he made noises, and he experimented, stringing noises together into "sentences." (Before any of his "words" made sense, he was using punctuation to make his babble sound like the adult babble around him.)

He began recognizing words and using them to mean the same thing to other people when they heard it as he meant when he said it. He progressed from "Dada" and "Mama" to "No!" and "Why?" and to hundreds of other words, phrases, and thoughts. He loved to listen to stories and to tell stories of his own.

Then teacher started Johnny over, at the beginning, trying to teach him how to read as if he had no idea how to use language at all.

"Look at Spot. See Spot run. Run Spot run. Funny, funny Spot."

No wonder so many of us had trouble learning how to read in school, even though so few of us had trouble learning how to talk.

beginning. I'll soon be able to keep up with you.

**6. Build on what I know.** This process is new to me, yes, but I know a lot about a lot of things.

When you teach me the new voice mail system, don't forget that I already know how to use a telephone.

When you teach me how to motivate a potential customer, don't forget that I was a customer for a lot of years before I started training to be a salesperson.

Use experience—yours and mine—to teach me. For example, do you handle that foot pedal the same way you feather the clutch on a car? Does the tug I'm supposed to feel when the gear engages feel anything like the way a trout feels on the line when it's mouthing the bait but hasn't swallowed the hook yet?

I may not understand the concept of jet propulsion, but I know what happens when you blow up a balloon and let it go without tying off the opening.

If you can explain what I don't know in terms of what I do know, I'll pick it up a lot faster. And if you aren't sure how much I know, I've got a simple suggestion: ask me. Let me show you what I know. If I'm doing it wrong—or in a way you don't want me to use—you'll see that, and we can work on it.

**7. Give me lots of feedback.** Tell me how I'm doing.

I'd prefer you told me nicely. You can skip the sarcasm, and you don't have to raise your voice. But however you do it, let me know if I'm doing it the way you want me to.

"Yes" is as important as "no." "Good job!" is just as helpful as "Not that way." Don't overdo the praise, and don't wait until I screw up to talk to me.

Don't just tell me what I'm doing wrong. Tell me how to do it right. In fact, if you just tell me how to do it right, you don't even have to bother telling me I'm wrong.

**8. Don't let it get away.** If you want me to really remember what we went over, give me another shot at it the same day, preferably about two hours after the first session. That will do me a lot more good than a review next week or even the next day. Reinforcing what I've learned promptly makes it stick.

**9. Let it all settle.** You did a great job, and I get it—I really do. But it seems to take a while for everything I learn to sink in. Don't make me tackle another new project right away. My subconscious needs to chew on this for a couple of hours before we move on to more new stuff.

## An Ideal Training Session

Now that you've heard about learning from your employees, let's take a look at the process again from your point of view. The following five steps provide a basic structure for any training session.

**Step 1. Lay it all out.** Explain the problem and the outcome you want.

**Step 2. Get them doing it.** The sooner workers get their hands on the task, the more involved they'll be, and the better they'll learn the process.

**Step 3. Give feedback as you go.** Anticipate and answer questions and guide the process each step of the way. Let them know how they're doing.

**Step 4. Give it a rest.** Let a tough lesson settle while workers do something relatively unchallenging.

**Step 5. Reinforce it.** Review the same day. It's best to review about two hours after the initial training session.

## How Will You Know If It Worked?

As with any other task in the workplace, you need a clear definition of what you want to accomplish in the training session and a way to evaluate whether you've accomplished it.

Before you started the training, you no doubt asked yourself, "What do I want or need to teach them?" Perhaps you also asked the more important question "What do I want them to learn?" You should also ask these two key questions:

- How will I know what they've learned?
- How should they act after the training?

With many processes, these questions are easy to answer. Either they can do it or they can't. They'll improve with practice. But if they're clearly on the right track, that's success.

However, other types of training are more difficult to evaluate. Quality training and sensitivity training fall into this category. Unfortunately, these types of training often fail, not for lack of good intentions but for lack of clear objectives and a way to measure or observe the results of the training.

Any time you plan to train workers, build into your plan a way to follow up. Keep it simple, and tell the learners what will be expected of them: "We'll try this again in a week to see how you do. I hope that you'll all be able to do it without any serious mistakes."

Discuss specific performance objectives and timelines with them. Don't end the training session until everybody knows what's supposed to happen next.

Training need not be formal, and it shouldn't be frightening—for you or for employees.

- Break the process down into manageable sections.
- Get them doing instead of just listening.
- Follow up.

You are the first and best source of on-the-job, on-the-spot training. Do your job well, and employees will grow in mastery, confidence, and productivity.

## The Coach's Checklist for Chapter 8

❑ Before you train others to do a task, make sure you have it mastered yourself.

❑ Break the process you want to teach into steps and keep them simple.

❑ Demonstrate how to do a task, then KYHO (keep your hands off) while the trainee begins to try to do it.

❑ Set up the training so the trainee experiences a series of small successes leading to the big success of mastery.

❑ Be empathetic with learners, show them respect, and help them build on what they know.

❑ Make sure you have a way to know whether learners have mastered the tasks you're training them in.

# The Coach
# as Mentor

"Frank," you say, looking him in the eye, "I normally don't give perfect performance evaluations. I've always believed you ought to leave a little room for improvement, even in the best employee. It's a motivator."

Frank looks dubious, waiting for his less-than-perfect work evaluation. "What did I do wrong?" his expression seems to ask.

"In your case," you continue, "I'm going to make an exception. Your work has been fantastic. I can always rely on you to do the job right the first time, and you often exceed my expectations."

Frank's face flushes, first with surprise, then pleasure. Clearly you've just exceeded his expectations.

"Thank you," he stammers.

"Not at all," you say. "You've earned it. That's why I'm so eager to help you find a better job elsewhere in the company."

Now Frank really looks surprised. What kind of manager would work to help his best employees leave his area?

A good coach, who puts the development of the individual first, might do just such a thing.

## Types of Mentoring

There are two kinds of mentoring. Both make sense for the
mentor, the employee, and the organization. Everybody wins
when you mentor effectively.

### Mentoring Within the Organization

As coach, you often must do more than simply train employees. You must show them how to get along in the workplace,
in the street sense. It's called "learning the ropes," and, like
the veteran boxer whose experience has taught him how large
the ring is and how to work the corners, the better your "fight-
ers" know the particular ring they work in, the better they'll
perform.

There's more to the job than just the job. Some of the most
important stuff never makes it into the personnel manual.

When you walk into the workplace for the first time, you
may encounter an invisible web of political intrigue and
ancient feuds. Maybe you stepped on a few land mines before
you got the lay of the land. Most of the rules aren't written
down. The "way we do things here" has evolved over years of
practice and tradition. Folks may not even know why they do
things the way they do.

Give the people who work with you the benefit of your
experience. Mentor them on the things they need to know to
flourish within the organization.

### Mentoring Outside the Organization

Its formal name is "career counseling," and it means helping
the individual chart long-term goals. Much of that kind of mentoring takes place within
the organization, of
course, as you show your
charges how their good
performance enables
them to advance within
the ranks by earning pro-
motions.

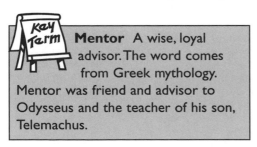

**Key Term**  **Mentor** A wise, loyal
advisor. The word comes
from Greek mythology.
Mentor was friend and advisor to
Odysseus and the teacher of his son,
Telemachus.

But some workers hit a wall, rising as high as they can without going someplace else. Sometimes that wall is you—for example, when your top lieutenant faces the prospect of waiting for you to advance, retire, or get a better job someplace else before being able to take your job.

You can try to keep the lid on those employees, hoping through material rewards like merit pay increases and symbolic ones like title changes, to keep them happy enough to stick with you, despite the lack of opportunity to grow.

Or you can help them move up and out.

Yes, you'll lose your organization's best employees that way. You'll have to recruit, hire, and train replacements. It will be a lot of work for you, with no guarantee that a new person will be as good as the one you lost.

And, yet, that's exactly what you should do.

If you don't help employees move on, you become an adversary. They see you as working against their best interests and that creates tension and distrust, making them more eager to move on. If a constricting economy limits opportunities elsewhere and you "succeed" in keeping that disgruntled employee, you no longer get peak performance, the goal of all coaching.

Effective mentoring can provide four important benefits:
1.  Employees who view a job with a sense of its possibilities become more motivated and productive.
2.  Employees will be loyal to you for as long as they work with you—and when they're working someplace else, too. (It never hurts to have friends.)
3.  Their advancement creates a vibrant working atmosphere, with everyone in the organization working to move up the ladder.
4.  You open up jobs in the organization that draw in new blood, new ideas, and new energy.

Balance these gains against the time it takes you to recruit and train new workers, and you will still come out way ahead.

## What It Takes to Be an Effective Mentor

The requirements are basic.

- Time
- Energy
- Willingness
- Accurate information

We've all got time and energy. It's just a matter of how we choose to spend them. Once you see how mentoring pays off for you, you'll put this important work ahead of some of the other things you do now.

You know how to get the information you don't already have. Remember, ignorance, your own or anybody else's, is a curable condition.

You've been gathering information since the day you started working. If you've worked your way up through the ranks, performing the jobs other people now do for you, you know the ins and outs as well as anybody.

Everybody has to learn to find his or her own way in the workplace. But you may be able to help members of your staff past some of the most obvious problems. Let's look at a few key areas to consider in your job as mentor.

### Coaching the In-Game

There's the process as it's outlined in the employees' manual, and then there's the way things really work.

Remember the questions you had when you were new to the job. Anticipate the problems a new employee will have. Head off the misunderstandings that result in somebody's not getting paid for their first month's work or filing for dental insurance after the cut-off date.

Who's supposed to sign off on the time sheets? What's the best time to apply for a job reclassification? How detailed do you have to be when you file for expenses?

The most important element in the in-game stems from the difference between the job description and the actual requirements of the job. Employees need to know what they're really expected to do and how you'll evaluate their work.

## Taking Emotional Temperatures

Some folks are quite open about expressing how they feel. But many more are apt to keep their feelings to themselves, especially when they're new to a job.

Don't wait for obvious signs of distress. Inquire after your workers' well being. Keep it casual, but don't let it ever become perfunctory.

"How's it going?" isn't fancy, but it's a fine question—if you ask it with genuine concern and a willingness to spend a little time listening to the answer. Without pushing or prodding, follow up if you suspect a problem: "Are you finding your way around OK?"

> **CAUTION!**
>
> ### Avoid Negativity
>
> When helping employees learn the in-game, be careful not to make them think that doing one thing but saying another is the norm. While managers in organizations don't always practice what they preach, avoid saying negative things about other people in the organization that will make those you're mentoring cynical or undermine their enthusiasm to perform well.

But some workers won't respond to what they perceive as being put on the spot. For them, you need to provide safe ways to express feelings and attitudes. The suggestion box has become a much belittled cliché, not because it's a bad idea, but because the concept has been abused by both sides. Too often, employees don't take the process seriously, refusing to offer suggestions or coming up with prank suggestions. Employers often ignore suggestions or, worse, seek to retaliate against employees who dare to offer suggestions they don't like.

Consider a variety of methods—including the suggestion box, surveys in employee newsletters, bulletin boards, e-mail postings, and drop-in office hours—to ensure employees ample opportunity to express their feelings.

You need this information. You can't coach without it.

## Coaching to Help People Move Forward

You might like to think that your staff members want to stay with you forever. And maybe your primary concern is their performance on the job at hand. You want the assistant junior management trainee to devote 100 percent to working at peak performance as an assistant junior management trainee. But she might have her eye on something a little better.

Would you really want a trainee who was content to be a trainee forever? Employees will do their best work for you now out of a strong motivation to move into a better opportunity later. Coach them for as long as you've got them, and help them, make realistic career plans. Then do whatever's necessary to make their plans work.

> **Smart Managing**
>
> ### Help Them Move Ahead
>
> If you have employees who learn quickly and have talent, think of part of your job as a coach as helping them move ahead. Give them opportunities to shine and take advantage of their talents. It will pay off for them, for you, and for the company.

Take advantage of job evaluation interviews and reviews to conduct formal mentoring. "You've been here three years already, Carol. It's time to consider putting in for a title change. I can give you the application and walk you through it if you'd like."

Also look for chances to mentor on the run. As with any type of coaching, much of your best mentoring will be unscheduled. Be ready to take advantage of opportunities.

## Applying the Principles of Basic Humanity

What if you must mentor someone who's older than you?

In many cultures, the young defer to the elders, acknowledging the wisdom only experience can teach and only age can confer. The assumption in such cultures is that the old mentor the young. Not so in America, where a 23-year-old manager may supervise a 73-year-old counter worker.

Apply the principles of basic humanity, regardless of age, culture, gender, or any other perceived difference. You have authority over the people who work with you. You will know more than they do in some situations. But remember: you aren't smarter, better, or more important than they are.

## Mentoring to Define the Work

Part of your job as mentor involves providing accurate, honest information and guidance about work expectations. This goes well beyond providing the job description, as we've noted, and it also goes beyond clarifying, explaining, and pointing out how the real job differs from the job on paper. You should also guide workers to positive, creative definitions of their jobs.

### Positive Definition of the Work

Somebody has to clean the bedpans in the nursing home. It isn't pleasant, it isn't ego-gratifying, and it isn't well-compensated.

You can call it "sanitation engineering," but don't tie a bow on it. It's still slinging bedpans.

Put the job in the context of the larger goal. Cleaning the bedpans is part of creating a healthy, pleasant environment for every resident of the nursing home. It's an important job, and it has positive, worthwhile outcomes.

### Creative Definition of the Work

A writer's life used to involve pounding out stories on a manual typewriter. That meant changing a lot of ink ribbons, wadding up a lot of paper, and slathering on a sea of Liquid Paper®. To get an extra copy, the writer had to insert a sheet of carbon paper between two sheets of typing paper, put the sandwich into the roller, and type harder.

Now writers type pixels on a screen and send the "words" as electronic impulses over a modem or push a button to print them out from a machine in another room. It's even common-place for books to be written online by writing partners who never meet face-to-face.

Writers who defined their job as typing words on paper locked themselves out of the profession long ago. Those writers who see their job as conveying information and telling stories have adapted well to this changing workplace. The tools are different, but not the ultimate product—understanding.

Mentors work to enable employees to define their jobs creatively—by ultimate purpose, not current tools—so that they'll develop the flexibility to adapt and survive.

## Mentoring to Motivate

You may need to channel the natural motivations workers bring with them to the workplace. This kind of mentoring often takes one of two forms: challenging the overachiever and getting the underachiever unstuck.

**Watch Out for Apathy**

Although the core problem is quite different, the symptom is the same: apathy.

The overachiever is bored because there's either not enough to do or nothing to do that provides challenge, stimulates learning, and results in meaningful productivity. The underachiever adopts boredom as a pose to mask insecurity.

One is wading, while the other is drowning. Both want to be swimming with the current, and both feel dissatisfied with their jobs.

You must look beneath the apathy and learn enough about the worker's abilities to be able to diagnose the problem accurately. Then you can apply the appropriate mentoring.

**1. The overachiever.** Forget pep talks and lectures. Don't set arbitrary goals or quotas. And don't create busy work. All these approaches will simply deepen the overachiever's dissatisfaction and may invite contempt.

Be open and honest, but not confrontational. Share your perception with the worker and discuss possible solutions.

Look for meaningful challenges. Set the bar a little higher, letting the worker succeed one level at a time. Provide additional training opportunities and give increasing amounts of responsibility. Ask the worker to play a leadership role in group settings.

**2. The underachiever.** Approach the underachiever as an

underused resource rather than as a problem. Workers don't want to disappoint you. They're motivated to do good work, and they want to be able to take pride in their work, just as you do.

Pep talks and lectures won't work here, either. Forget carrots and sticks. Again, get the worker involved in dialog.

Together you may be able to create a better match of worker and task. Explore possibilities for altering the work environment or routine to get rid of stumbling blocks.

> **No Excuses Needed**
>
> If there's no fault, there's no need for excuses.
>
> You aren't looking for something or someone to blame. You're looking for ways to help a worker do a job better. With that approach, you're working together, with a common goal. The worker will see you as an ally, not a threat.

As with all coaching opportunities, set some guidelines, a way to measure progress, and arrange for a follow-up session.

## Respecting the Boundaries of Mentoring

You're a manager, a coach, a mentor. You motivate and guide. You make decisions, evaluate performance, solve problems.

You do not "fix" psychological problems or mediate disputes for one simple reason: *You aren't qualified to deal with them.*

If you've got a "dysfunctional" department, clearly in need of some group therapy, you've got two alternatives:

- **Bring in an expert.** If your organization is large enough to have an Office of Employee Assistance or a similar department, arrange to have a professional come in, help you establish guidelines, and conduct an extended discussion or series of discussions to work through problems. If you don't have an in-house pro, look to the nearest university extension or outreach program. Many have experts on conflict resolution in the workplace who will work with you for reasonable fees. Hold such sessions away from the workplace, but don't call them "retreats" or half of the workers will hate the process before they ever get started.

- **Create firm boundaries.** If you can't solve the problem, as leader you must enforce a cease-fire. Admit that you can't "fix" things. Don't pretend to be fair. Discuss, develop, and implement guidelines for behavior. Nobody will be happy. They'll all blame you. But at least they'll be united in that, and you'll be able to get some work done.

Despite the problems inherent in mentoring employees, most of your mentoring will be positive and productive. Combined with training and problem solving, it will help move your staff closer to peak performance.

## The Coach's Checklist for Chapter 9

❏ There are two types of mentoring: inside the organization and outside the organization. One teaches skills and organizational savvy; the other helps a person build a career.

❏ To be a successful mentor, you need to have the time, energy, willingness, and accurate information to share.

❏ Mentoring involves helping people understand how things are "really done around here."

❏ Successful mentors understand that they are no smarter, better, or more important than anyone else. They understand their role as a helper, however, and they take it seriously.

❏ Mentors help people understand their work not as tasks but as contributions to a process to deliver an output others will value.

❏ Mentors help bolster employee motivation.

**10**

# The Coach
# as Corrector

Training employees for new procedures, teaching them new
skills, and helping them map out a career path are positive
roles for a coach.

Having to correct inadequate performance and unacceptable behavior in the workplace is more difficult. In this chapter,
we'll discuss some principles that will help you take the sting
out of the encounter and make it productive rather than punitive.

## Make It an Encounter,
## Not a Confrontation

Your attitude going into
the situation will in large
part determine your suc-
cess or failure. Take a
positive, goal-oriented
approach. The goal, as
always, is better employ-
ee performance.

First, focus on the
behavior, not the person.
Avoid talking about a per-

**They React to You**

**CAUTION!**

Before you begin
addressing a worker's behavior,
recognize your part in the relationship and that the worker may in part
be reacting to your actions. You may
be able to eliminate all or part of the
problem by becoming aware of the
signals you're giving off through your
words and deeds.

Your behavior is a lot easier for
you to change than anybody else's.
Check it out first.

son's tendencies, characteristics, or traits. Focus on specific actions and outcomes and how they need to change.

For example, Jan has been arriving at work from 10 minutes to a half an hour late three or four days a week for three weeks. Employees don't have to punch a time clock, but they're expected to keep regular hours, and your company frowns on workers taking comp time unless a supervisor approves it in advance.

Rather than send around a memo warning everyone to get to work on time, you decide to call Jan in for some coaching. Good decision. You're already way ahead of the game.

### Don't Generalize

If you treat an individual situation as if it were a general problem, you risk causing resentment, rumors, or even an epidemic.

When you generalize your reaction, other employees may resent the "troublemaker." If they don't know who the troublemaker is, they may guess at the culprit and spread rumors. Or they may even decide that there's no advantage in avoiding trouble, because you lump the good and the bad together. So, by generalizing your correction, you may be spreading the problem you're trying to resolve.

No matter what your tone of voice, if you open the discussion with "You seem to have trouble getting to work on time," it will sound like an accusation (because that's what it is). Jan is apt to react defensively, with a denial, an excuse, or withdrawal. You'll lecture. She'll seethe. You'll accomplish nothing positive. The problem is that you focused on Jan, labeling her as chronically late.

Here's how to start the conversation with the focus on the *behavior* rather than the *person*: "I've noticed that you've been getting to work late."

Jan might still react defensively, but you have a much better basis for discussion, especially if you make it clear that you're looking for solutions: "Is there anything we can do about that?"

Second, focus on the specific, not the general. Avoid

"always" and "never," as in "You're always late" or "You're never on time." Either way, you've made a sweeping general-ization—which simply turns the truth into an exaggeration, a lie. Since it's an exaggeration, it's impossible to prove it—and foolish to try.

You'll have to back down from the generalization, if you're wise. But you'll then likely start quibbling about small points, in order to make some sort of case. Even if you win the debate, you'll lose ground in your relationship with Jan. You may succeed in getting her to arrive at work on time, but that may be a hollow victory.

Specific is better. Present your observation to Jan, giving her detailed information about the problem as you see it: "You've been getting to work anywhere from 10 minutes to a half an hour late three or four days a week." If you start like that, you'll be talking about specific behaviors rather than gen-eralizations or character traits.

You're a coach, not a cop. You're seeking performance, not punishment. You need to do what works, not what feels good.

## Apply the PSA Formula: Positive Specific Action

Aim for change, not blame. Don't simply tell an employee what not to do. Always coach toward positive behaviors. What is the employee *supposed* to do?

The way you describe the problem (character flaw, chronic condition, or specific behavior) is crucial. After you've defined the behavior, you want to talk about it as specifically as you can, following up with these two steps:

**Step 1. State why the behavior needs changing.** This first step might seem obvious to you. You *assume* employees know why they shouldn't arrive late for work, for example. But assumptions seldom make for effective communication. In all but the most obvious situations, you need to be clear and spe-cific as to why the behavior needs changing.

Aside from the fact that Jan's lateness cheats the system and angers her co-workers—who are looking to you to be fair—how does Jan's lateness affect the work (hers and oth-

**Prepare Your Reasoning**

Prepare your reasoning before you meet with the employee. First, write down all your reasons why you want to correct the behavior. Then, try to look at each of your reasons from other points of view. What seems logical or reasonable or necessary from your perspective may not seem so to the employee.

If your list of reasons gets reduced to something like "because it's company policy" or "because that's how I like to run my department," you may want to think about the situation a little more before you meet with the employee.

ers)? The more specific you are here, the more likely it is that Jan will buy into your viewpoint and change her behavior.

**Step 2. Ask a question that points toward a solution.** This question can take many forms, depending on several factors—the problem, the situation, and your relationship with the employee. In some instances, you might simply shrug your shoulders or raise an eyebrow.

What might most effectively open up a discussion of possible solutions? And who should be responsible for suggesting solutions? You may choose to put the burden

- on the employee ("What can you do to keep this from happening again?"),
- on both of you (" Is there something I can do to help?"), or
- on the process ("How can we work this out?").

In many cases, the process approach will yield the best results.

Sticking to PSA will force you to think before you coach, and that will make you a better coach.

## Define Consequences Clearly

You need to be clear about what's at stake.

The trickiest part of any attempt to change someone's behavior comes when you confront the "Or else?" question. Whether the employee asks or not, you need to be very clear about the consequences, the "or else."

First, be specific. Vague mumblings to "shape up or ship out" or warnings that "we could have a bigger problem" accomplish nothing—except making you look ineffectual. High-sounding language about "dire repercussions and sanctions" is no better—just more pompous. State potential consequences specifically.

Second, avoid a threatening tone. Your goal is to change the behavior, not to punish the employee. Make sure your tone as well as your words convey your focus on this goal.

Finally, never invoke a consequence that won't happen. We all learned a long time ago to disregard phony warnings and other threatened punishments that never came to pass.

You should have specific procedures in place for dealing with inadequate performance and unacceptable workplace behavior.

---

### Actions and Consequences

As much as possible, the consequences you cite should arise naturally from the actions, rather than being imposed. It's better to talk about your concern that the team might not complete certain tasks or meet its performance goals or reach its objectives, rather than about sanctions such as docked pay.

If you can't come up with any specific consequences in terms of performance, you may be dealing with a behavior you'd be better off overlooking. Again, that decision depends on the employee and your relationship. You may be able to correct behavior simply by showing your concern or by making some adjustments.

---

Such procedures outline sequential steps, typically moving from verbal warning through written reprimand to a letter in the personnel file. Further problems may result in suspension, demotion, and, ultimately, termination.

You need to know the organization's procedures and your authority within them. Failure to follow the procedures is unfair and, in most cases, illegal.

So, don't say it unless you're prepared to back it up. If you don't follow through this time, your words won't have much influence the next time—or perhaps with other employees.

## Build on the Possible

Is it really a behavior problem?

You may be assuming that the employee *won't*. Consider the possibility that she or he *can't*—but doesn't want you to know it.

Take me, for example, coach. No matter how many times you tell me, no matter how often you show me, and no matter how much you threaten punishment if I fail, or promise rewards if I succeed, I'm never going to be able to dunk a basketball (except in my dreams, of course).

Can't you let me do something else, instead? I'm really good at shooting free throws. I know I can help the team that way.

Start with what an employee can do and work toward what she or he isn't doing yet.

Begin formal and informal performance evaluations with strengths, not weaknesses. Whenever possible, emphasize those strengths by allowing employees to do more of what they do well, leading them by steps into increasingly difficult and more complex tasks.

And sometimes folks work better in teams, even while each performs a solo task. If you partner a struggling worker with a confident, capable one, you may help the first worker improve performance.

You may recognize the benefits of natural cross-training here. Employees who work as partners or in teams tend to know more about what the other partners or the teammates are doing. That makes it easier if you need to shift responsibilities when somebody's absent or if job demands suddenly change.

Remember: one size does *not* fit all, and one formula for measuring productivity can't adequately measure every worker's performance. Your goal must be to bring each employee to his or her peak level of performance—or as close to it as possible—not to an arbitrary performance standard for all employees. (Not to mention standards for other areas of behavior.)

Even if compensation is based on an absolute scale—as when an employee is paid per project completed or unit sold—you must evaluate each employee by an individual and subjective scale. Treating all employees fairly, acknowledging what's possible for them to achieve, doesn't mean treating them all the same.

## Look to the Future

You want results, not excuses. What counts is what the employee does next.

Be clear about how past performance or behavior has failed to meet expectations. But once you've done this, move on to specific goals. Let the past go. Don't hold grudges (in your head or in the employee's personnel folder). Give employees the chance to make it right and get beyond the problem.

## Performance Killers

Here are some correction methods that will guarantee failure in any attempts to correct poor performance or unacceptable behavior in employees. For discussion purposes, we'll group these methods under three general headings: false judgment, false solution, and avoidance.

### False Judgment
- Diagnosing
- Psychoanalyzing
- Labeling/stereotyping
- Non-specific praising/supporting

There's a big difference between judging the behavior or performance of a worker and judging the worker as a person.

Avoid diagnosing ("Your basic problem is a bad attitude") and psychoanalyzing ("You've got a problem accepting a male authority figure because your Dad died when you were 11"). You don't have the necessary training or enough information to make such characterizations. They'll just get in your way as you try to deal with an employee.

You'd never consider applying a racial, ethnic, or gender stereotype to a worker. (No need to offer examples here. Unfortunately, we're all only too familiar with prejudices.) But watch out for more subtle stereotypes (the way "those people" think or behave). Any conclusion based on a categorical generalization, such as age, educational background, clothing, or anything else, will erode your ability to coach.

Even such positive reinforcement as praise can make you a less effective coach, if it's based on generalizations. The statement "You've got an MBA, so you must really know your stuff" is just as likely to be wrong as "You're doing well for a woman." You should also be careful that your praise doesn't convey a feeling of surprise, as if you had lower expectations for an employee: "Wow! Great job tightening that bolt!" might be taken as meaning "You've got a scraggly beard and long hair and an earring, so I was wondering what kind of work we could get out of you." Sometimes it is just a subtle matter of not praising excessively.

> **MISTAKE PROOFING**
>
> ### Assume with Care
>
> All managers understand the need to be sensitive to differences among employees, right? And sometimes those differences are easier to notice because of race, ethnicity, or gender, right?
>
> Yes, but here you may start to slip into a dangerous area. You should be *sensitive* to differences but should avoid *assuming* differences. Especially be careful to avoid assuming that anything that makes an individual different will necessarily affect that person's behavior or performance.

## False Solution

- Cracker barrel philosophy
- Morality tales

• Unsolicited advice

"To thine own self be true," Polonius advises his son, Laertes, in William Shakespeare's immortal classic *Hamlet,* "and it follows as the night the day, you must be true to all men."

Sage advice from a wise elder? Then why did audiences at the old Globe Theatre snicker when they heard those words?

Folks in Shakespeare's day called such

> **Opinions Matter**
>
> Voicing a negative judgment may bring swift, negative reaction. But just holding the negative opinion, even if you never state or overtly act on it, hurts you as a manager. Your false assumptions make you less aware of a worker's abilities and muddle your ability to make decisions.
>
> Yes, it's still a free country and you have a right to your opinions. But on the job you're responsible for being a good manager. And what good manager underestimates assets and undermines decision making?

windy pontifications "copy book wisdom," because school children copied the phrases to practice their penmanship. Polonius was being no wiser than the sharpie who advises you not to take any wooden nickels. The advice is true. It's just tired and often not all that helpful.

Even if your words of wisdom came from your mom and dad rather than Shakespeare, workers may not want or need to hear them.

That's true whether you're quoting Polonius or telling the tale of the ant and the grasshopper or sharing an experience from your past. Don't assume that employees will be interested in your story or find it helpful. Think about your sage words, your tales of wisdom, and the lessons you've learned along life's path. If you truly believe that something will help employees develop, share it. If not, save it for a more appropriate occasion.

That brings us to the final performance killer in this section: unsolicited advice.

If you find yourself starting a sentence with "This is really none of my business," your next words should not be "but if you ask me ...." Try saying "so I'll keep my mouth shut" instead. Then do it. If that employee is curious, she'll ask. (But be careful to avoid intimidating her into asking.)

## Avoidance

- Diversion
- The old bob and weave
- Later
- False assurance

Refusing to deal with an issue may buy you a little time, but it will also likely make the situation worse. The longer you allow poor performance or unacceptable behavior to continue, the more reinforced and established that behavior becomes. Your silence sends employees the message that you approve of the behavior or at least accept it.

The employees who are guilty of the poor performance or unacceptable behavior then feel free to continue, while others might let their performance slide or worry less about their behavior. And your problem just grows.

Don't keep changing the subject. Diversion is not a solution. Deal with it.

Another classic avoidance technique is "the old bob and weave." We invite you now to watch a performance by experts (a veteran reporter trying to pin down an equally veteran politician).

As we join the program already in progress, the reporter wants to confirm rumors (based on "usually reliable" but unnamed sources, of course) that the politician has sexually harassed a campaign worker. Knowing that any reply on the subject will hurt him, the politician attempts to divert by seeming to take the high ground.

**Reporter** (looking concerned and serious): "Sir, how would you respond to the disturbing reports regarding your sexual misconduct during the recent campaign?"

**Politician** (smiling broadly and nodding): "I appreciate your question. But you know, the real issue facing the American people (turning a sincere gaze to the camera) is the lack of adequate health care protection for over 40 percent of working Americans today. Now, the bill I have just placed before Congress...."

This dance can go on forever. The reporter talks about inappropriate touching, while the politician talks about his push for appropriations.

The next avoidance technique on the list is "later," as in "never, if I'm lucky." Managers often slip out from under a problem by thinking, like poor doomed Scarlet O'Hara in the classic tale *Gone With the Wind*, "Tomorrow's another day."

You really should talk to Geoff about his poor performance, but you dread the task. You have a lot of "real" work to do, after all, and surely another day won't hurt.

But another day will hurt. Tomorrow turns into today, and you're even less willing and able to face the difficult confrontation. Time may heal all wounds, but it doesn't solve most performance and behavior problems in the workplace. They won't usually be "gone with the wind."

False assurance can be as harmful as any other form of avoidance. "Nothing to worry about," you tell the worker grandly. "This thing will work itself out." The worker leaves feeling better—or not, depending on how much trust you've earned—while the problem continues to grow.

Don't let any of these performance killers get in your way. They're all evasions of your responsibility to confront poor performance.

Workers are responsible for the consequences of their actions. But as a supervisor, you're responsible for managing their performance. Even if they're at fault, you must take responsibility for improving the situation.

As coach, you must be problem solver, trainer, teacher, mentor, and corrector. Prepare for all these roles, and approach each with a positive, goal-oriented attitude. No matter what the role, your ultimate goal must always be the same: helping the worker achieve peak performance.

No matter how firm your resolve to accept this responsibility and to tackle problems head on, some basic characteristics of the human beings you work with might get in your way as you attempt to become an effective coach. We'll discuss those potential pitfalls—and solutions to them—in the next chapter.

## The Coach's Checklist for Chapter 10

❏ When you're correcting employees, remember to make it an encounter, not a confrontation.

❏ Avoid accusing the employee; just examine the specific behaviors and try to understand them and their causes together.

❏ Use the Positive Specific Action (PSA) model to help employees improve their behavior. This includes defining the behavior and why it needs to change and asking questions that lead to a solution, and then agreeing on that solution.

❏ If change doesn't happen let the employee know the specific consequences of that.

❏ Make sure the employees have the capabilities to do what's asked. And don't assume they do without checking on that.

❏ Once you've dealt with the problem, let the past go and look to the future—that's better for the coach and the employee.

❏ Performance killers include making false judgments, coming up with false solutions, and trying to avoid the problem.

# Coaching
# Land Mines

Good intentions alone won't make you a good coach. Even applying all the great advice from the first 10 chapters of this book aren't enough to get the job done if you fall into any of the potential traps we'll discuss in this chapter.

These coaching land mines can be hard to spot, but once you locate them they're easy to avoid.

## Lack of Authentic Purpose

A dog will often circle—sometimes several times—before settling down to sleep. The most popular explanation for this is that it's a defensive behavior left over from wilderness days. The dog circles to get a 360° look at the surroundings to make sure no enemies are near. The fact that dogs sense the presence of other creatures primarily through smell, not sight, seems to weaken the theory.

Basically, dogs circle because that's what dogs do. Dogs circle, owls hoot, and washing your car makes it rain. It's just the way things are.

You and your workers may be doing a bit of circling before you sit down in the workplace, too, for reasons nobody remembers, assuming anybody knew in the first place.

When you first study the principles of time management,

you may be amazed at how often you'll catch yourself performing tasks that have no clear benefit to you or to anybody
else, simply because you did them the day before, and the day
before that, and the day before....

Make sure your management behaviors never fall into that
category. Have a purpose for everything you do. Remind yourself not only of what you should do but of what you hope to
accomplish by doing it.

Here are three ways to avoid performing purposeless activities.

**1. Don't just do it to be doing it.** People do certain things
because they've always done them. They do them because the
person who had the job before them did those things. They do
them because someone told them to (or they read it in a management book). They do them so that someone will see them
doing those things. And they do them so that they can say
they did them.

None of these are good reasons to do anything. Look for
the real reason behind the practice—and abandon it if it does
not serve a useful purpose.

**2. Don't mistake the activity for the results.** Does the rooster
really believe that his lusty crowing makes the sun rise?

When people link cause and effect erroneously (as when
the baseball player refuses to wash his "lucky" socks during a
hitting streak), it's called superstition. In the workplace, it's
called a waste of time. But people don't always spot erroneous
cause-and-effect links. So, they go on mistaking an activity
(such as scanning a page of print) with the desired result
(making sense of the words on the page), resulting in the non-
sensical assertion that "Yeah, I read it, but I didn't understand it."

The goal is peak performance. If quality circles help
employees perform better, then have quality circles. But quality circles—and meetings, committees, reports, memos, phone
calls, and training sessions—must never become an end in
themselves. They must always be the means to some clear
goal. If the activity doesn't get you the result you want, do
something else.

**3. Keep it relevant.** Most people would rather be busy than bored, active than idle. It feels good to produce, especially when the output is tangible.

Writers feel a sense of well-being as the computer screen fills with words. But they don't get paid for filling screens with words; they get paid for writing something that other people want or need to read. That involves thinking, and sometimes the thinking requires that they stop "making progress" at the computer screen and instead spend some time staring, pacing, and muttering.

Never mistake *motion* for *progress*. You may be making great time, but if you're heading in the wrong direction, your speed is only taking you further from your goal.

---

**Busy** You don't really need a definition of this word, do you? But so often people, especially managers, feel that "busy" is a synonym of "Important."
How often do you hear the following dialogs?
*Dialog 1*
John: "Hey, boss! Have you got a minute?"
Mary: "Not now. I'm busy."
*Dialog 2*
Bill: "Hey, Mary. Have you got a minute?"
Mary: "Of course!"
The two dialogs occurred within 30 seconds. Mary was busy one moment, then the next moment she could spare some time. What happened? Simple: position. John works for Mary, while Mary works for Bill. Mary was too busy (important) for John, but not too busy (important) for Bill.
Take your "work pulse" from time to time. Are you using "busy" as if it really means "important"? Remember: it's good to be busy with important things, but it's bad to be busy doing things to be important.

---

## Anxiety (Yours)

No one likes to admit it, but most people experience anxiety in their day-to-day dealings with others. The anxiety can become especially acute when they must deliver bad news, correct unacceptable behavior, improve inadequate performance, or many of the other tasks that often burden a manager.

Anxiety is natural and unavoidable. It can even be helpful if you can focus and channel the anxiety as energy available to help you do the job.

The first step in dealing with anxiety, then, is simply to admit you've got it. Then decide if you can harness that energy or if you need to work on reducing it.

Nothing combats anxiety better than preparation. Some managers choose to prepare obsessively, to make sure that everything is planned carefully, down to the last detail. But

**TRICKS OF THE TRADE**

### Back-of-the-Business-Card

Whatever the cause of your anxiety, you can often apply the back-of-the-business-card technique to get ready to tackle it.

Take your business card, turn it over, and write no more than three key words or phrases that outline the steps you need to take or the points you need to make. Save a little space to note exactly when you'll take these steps.

If you can do this well in advance of the stressful situation, carry the card around with you so that you can take it out and glance at it whenever the anxiety returns. As the moment approaches, allow yourself one more "rehearsal" by reviewing your points.

This technique works even when you have only a couple of minutes to prepare. It will ease your anxiety and improve your performance every time.

sometimes you just don't have that much time to prepare. And sometimes all that preparation can hurt you if you encounter something unexpected—such as an unusual question, a mechanical glitch, or a last-minute schedule change.

What if you can't prepare? How do you deal with anxiety?

Here's a little lesson from Linus. He deals with the anxieties of his world by carrying around his security blanket. Whatever happens, he can fight the anxiety by holding his blanket close.

What works for Linus might work for you. No, I'm not proposing that you carry around a blanket. But you might try keeping something in your pocket that will give you a lift, inspire you, remind you of what really matters to you. It could be a picture of someone you love, a lucky penny, a pebble that reminds you of a vacation by the sea, or the keys to your Porsche.

What do you miss most when you're at work? What makes you feel most at ease when you leave the office? Carrying a piece of that good feeling may help you through your times of anxiety.

## Fear/Distrust (Theirs)

Employees may be afraid of you or distrust you simply because you're the boss. It's nothing personal, but if you sit in the boss's chair, behind the boss's desk, you evoke boss feelings.

Although that's not your fault, you need to take responsibility for managing their fear and distrust.

The fear may wear many disguises. It may cause employees to react defensively, to be excessively deferential, to frequently make excuses, and to avoid you. On the theory that the best defense is a strong offense, some employees may challenge your authority in various ways, acting out their fear aggressively.

Many frightened people adopt an unconscious strategy called passive resistance. When you coach them, they nod pleasantly and mumble agreement. They just don't do what you told them to do, because they're afraid to displease you by doing it wrong.

Once you become aware that fear is motivating any employee, you can begin to combat that fear.

The first step is to acknowledge that you might be doing something to create or nurture the fear. Examine your own behaviors for anything that might appear threatening, even though you don't intend it that way.

Once you've removed any potentially threatening behav-

## Be Aware ... of Yourself!

Bill was the president of a small company. He tried hard to be friendly toward all his employees, but he was unaware that he was constantly undermining those efforts.

Bill was a large man with a big voice. When he sat, he tended to sprawl. When he spoke, it was with volume. Unfortunately, he also had a monotone voice.

When he met with employees or managers, he didn't realize that some of them felt intimidated, as much by those aspects of his physical presence as by his position as president. If he made a statement, they felt he was laying down the law. If he asked a few questions, they felt that he was giving them the third degree. Even his casual attitude, which should have been an asset, worked against him—his informality was interpreted as a lack of respect.

What was Bill doing to inspire fear? Nothing but being himself. But he was guilty of not being self-aware—and many people suffered, including Bill.

iors, work quietly to overcome employee fear by offering genuine assurance. Something as simple as a smile can be enormously helpful here.

(Of course, we don't need to tell you to not do anything to punish a fearful employee. Don't even say anything about it. No matter how kind your intentions, making a reassuring comment such as "Well, now, I hope you're not so scared of me anymore" punishes the employee.)

**CAUTION!**

### It's Not All Your Fault

Behavior you identify as passive resistance may stem from fear, but you may not be the cause. Employees come to the job not only fears but personal hostilities and idiosyncrasies. So, while some of their feelings may relate to you and your behaviors and you may be able to address them, others have nothing to do with you and, if they don't affect employee performance, are none of your business.

## Resistance to Change

Most people resist change—in their routines and patterns, the way they think, and the assumptions they hold.

Here's a quick exercise to demonstrate why

habits are so hard to break. Clasp your hands. Now unclasp
and clasp again. Which thumb is on top? Now clasp your
hands again, this time making sure the "wrong" thumb winds
up on top. Cheap thrills, eh?

If you're like most
folks, this requires a little
thought, and It feels awk-
ward. The same thing will
happen if you take the
"wrong" shoe off first
when you undress tonight
or start in the "wrong"
quadrant of your mouth
when you brush your
teeth. People are creatures
of habit, and any other but
the habitual way of doing
things can feel downright weird.

### It Isn't Personal

Don't take the resis-
tance personally.

If you're initiating changes, it's natural to think the resistance is a reaction to you. But remember that it's
the changes they're resisting, not you
or your authority. Work through the
changes together, stressing your common goals and the reasons why the
changes will help all of you reach
those goals.

When you coach an employee toward peak performance,
you may challenge well-established habits and thought patterns. When you adopt new coaching strategies, you disrupt
your own sense of well-being and balance.

First acknowledge this resistance in yourself and others.
Look past the initial unwillingness to try, the automatic "no."
Be patient, with yourself and with others. Acknowledge and
allow for backsliding. The moment you stop concentrating on
what you're doing, you'll revert to old patterns. Give yourself
and employees time to establish new patterns.

## Lack of Coaching Skills

Think of something you do well. Perhaps you're a better-than-
average bridge player, possess a dangerous backhand on the
tennis court, can whip up a mean stir fry, or have the touch to
lay a dry fly just upstream from a feeding trout. You weren't
born with these skills. You had to first learn and then develop
them.

> ⚠️ **CAUTION!**
>
> ## Ghosts of Teachers Past
>
> Most of us have known some bad teachers or at least had some bad experiences with teachers. Over the years, we've left them behind—or so we believe. But memories of them can interfere with how we learn later in life.
>
> Perhaps the worst-case scenario is that of an employee who once had a terrible teacher, somebody who made him feel stupid, and he disliked school from then on. Now, years out of school, he's still having trouble learning, because he's nagged by those memories and the self-doubt from years past. He might not be fully conscious of the effects of that bad teacher or be able to express them, but he feels them.
>
> What can you do? Be sensitive, be caring, be the best coach you can be, but don't be surprised if you encounter image problems.

You weren't born with all the skills you need to be an effective coach, either. And some of the behaviors might not come naturally to you. Acknowledge and work on (or around) your weaknesses. It's just as important to celebrate your strengths and build on them. Note your progress as you continue to become a better coach.

Workers may lack the skills they need to receive coaching effectively. They may have never experienced a manager who discusses problems and procedures with them and values their input. They may not know how to participate in problem solving.

Don't assume that either you or the worker will take to a procedure naturally. You both might have to work at it. That will help, not hinder, the process—so long as you work together.

Explain what you're doing and why. Admit your own uncertainties about the changes. Then learn the processes together.

## The Language Barrier

Aquì se habla coaching? If you speak only English, and your employee speaks only Spanish, you know you've got a communication problem, and you must work to solve it. That may not be easy, but at least you recognize the communication barrier.

But what about the invisible language barrier? That's when you both think you're speaking the same language, but you're not communicating. You may have a problem and not even realize it.

Two types of language barriers can block effective communication between you and an employee—jargon and assumption.

**1. The jargon barrier.** If your third base coach ordered you to put down a suicide squeeze, would you know what you were supposed to do?

You would if you understood baseball jargon. You're being instructed to bunt the next pitch, preferably hard enough to get it past the charging first and third basemen. The runner at third will be breaking for the plate as soon as the pitcher releases the ball. If you don't make contact with the ball, he'll be an easy out. But you can't hit it hard enough that the charging infielders have a play at home. Got it now?

Each sport has its own jargon. So do all hobbies and professions. Most of us wouldn't know a butterfly stitch from a Butterball turkey, but any good medical intern knows what it is and how to tie one.

> **Watch the Jargon**
>
> If employees don't understand your jargon, they may think you're trying to impress them or to disguise your weaknesses. Either way—you're not only putting up barriers to effective communication, you're also damaging your relationship with them.
>
> Smart Managing

Managers develop jargon, too, and then forget that the rest of the world doesn't understand their language—and may have no interest in learning it. Don't bury your workers in phrases from your last management seminar unless you're willing and able to translate and unless they have some need to know the terminology. If not, stick with a language you both understand.

**2. The assumption barrier.** People use language just as they use money. They exchange words and they exchange currency, trusting in a shared understanding of the value of both words and money. After all, a dollar is a dollar, right? Not quite.

What would you do for a dollar? Probably not much: it's just change to you. But to an eight-year-old, it might mean a great trip to the candy store.

How about $10,000? Now you're interested—but would it interest Bill Gates, Donald Trump, and Ted Turner? It might not even buy a decent suit.

Similarly, everyone knows the face value of words (more or less), but individuals tend to have different values for many words.

Take "ASAP," for example. Most folks can tell you that "ASAP" stands for "as soon as possible" and that it means "Do it right away." But if you tell an employee to get the job done ASAP, you may mean "within the next five minutes" or "before I get back from lunch," but the employee may think you mean "as soon as you get done with what you're working on now" or "before you go home this afternoon."

Such common coinage can be dangerous because both sender and receiver assume they know what it means. Only later do they discover that their assumptions didn't match.

If you need it done before lunch, say so.

## Coaching Chokers

In this category, we'll take on a handful of some of the more minor, but still troublesome, land mines you may find along the road to effective coaching.

### The One-Way Street

If you're doing all the communicating, you may not be communicating at all.

Written communication and voice mail messages carry an obvious danger: without feedback from the receivers, you have no way of knowing if they've gotten, let alone understood what you said. If they don't respond, you might think that they don't

like what you said or that they don't agree with it. If you react
to that assumption, you could really mess things up.

Even face-to-face communication can be deceptive. Workers may appear to listen attentively, even nod in seeming comprehension, smile and say "Yep" at all the right places—and
still have no idea what you're talking about.

Why don't they just ask? Because they don't want to look
stupid in your eyes. As children, we all learned to bluff in
school, where looking confused can draw the teacher's fire.

Ask for questions and, of course, be open to them. But you
must do more. Rather than passively waiting for the listener to
indicate a lack of understanding, provide specific information
and then actively seek confirmation of understanding. For
example, when you finish a series of complicated instructions,
follow them up with "Now, tell me what you're going to do."

### The Interrogation

When the homicide detective on TV says, "These are just routine questions," the poor subject is in serious trouble.

Asking good questions and then listening actively to the
answers are two of your best coaching tools. But you misuse
and abuse the technique when questioning becomes the third
degree.

Avoid asking questions in staccato bursts, and avoid
rhetorical questions, fill-in-the-blank questions, and pointed
questions.

- **Rhetorical questions** come with a built-in right answer.
  When the insurance sales representative asks if you want
  to be sure that your family is adequately protected when
  you're no longer able to bring home a paycheck, you
  know you're not supposed to say "no." The rep is trying
  to get that first "yes" response to involve you in the sales
  pitch.

  Rhetorical questions are manipulative and don't repre-
  sent honest communication. They may get you hostility
  instead of dialog and cooperation.
- **Fill-in-the-blank questions** treat the person giving the

answers like a somewhat slow fifth-grader, struggling to pass a quiz.

"Who can tell us the land mines to effective coaching discussed in this chapter? Someone? Anyone?"

Pretty simple stuff, if you limit your questions to that level. It's hardly the kind of probe that would encourage a worker to enter into a serious discussion.

- **Pointed questions**, like their rhetorical cousins, also carry their own implied "right" answers: "You wouldn't really want to do that, *would* you?" A worker wouldn't even have to know what you're talking about to know that you don't think she ought to do it.

Ask *real* questions that need *real* answers, and you'll do fine.

## Focus on Fixing

An employee brings you a problem, and you fix it. That's your job, right?

Yes. And no.

Making sure the job gets done is part of your job. However, coaching employees to peak performance is the larger, more important part of your job.

It may take a bit more time—and a lot more patience—to coach employees to fix problems rather than to take the problems out of their hands and do the fixing yourself. But in the long run, you'll wind up "fixing" the same problem time after time, all the while nurturing frustration and dependence in employees.

## The Blame Game

"Hey, boss. The copy machine's jammed again."

"Who fouled it up this time?!"

Instead of fixing it yourself or, better still, coaching the employee to fix it, you spend your time and energy trying to figure out whose fault it is. You wind up with two frustrated people—you and the employee. You may or may not know who gets the blame, and you haven't done a thing to solve the problem.

### Failure to Follow Through

Follow-through is crucial in golf, tennis, and coaching.

When you give an assignment, establish clear criteria for evaluating progress and set a time for a follow-up session. In less formal situations, jot yourself a reminder to check on a worker's progress. Don't wait until the product's past due to go looking for the producer.

You've got the tools you need to handle problems, to prevent problems from happening, and to turn negatives into positives.

In the next chapter, we'll take a close look at your role as a problem solver, examining a specific coaching session by breaking it down into seven component parts.

## The Coach's Checklist for Chapter 11

❑ Eliminate activities that no longer have a purpose. They undermine your effectiveness and that of your employees as well.

❑ You can't avoid anxiety at times, so recognize it and develop a personal method for handling it rather than letting it handle you.

❑ Examine your behavior and attitude. Make sure you aren't doing things that will strike fear into your employees. Fear gets in the way of communication and performance—yours and theirs.

❑ Understand why people (including you) resist change, and you can deal with the resistance successfully, to everyone's benefit.

❑ Make sure your employees really understand what you're saying. Don't use language and jargon that gets in the way of communicating clearly.

❑ Avoid one-way communication, interrogations, and the urge to personally fix all problems.

# Steps to Effective Coaching

As a manager, you're responsible for making sure that the work gets done promptly and properly. That's what "managing" means.

But for a supervisor who manages by coaching, getting the work done is only part of the job. The other part, often the more important part, is developing employees to be able to function effectively and independently.

Here's a simple process to help you do both:

**Step 1.** Name the challenge and describe the desired outcome.

**Step 2.** Brainstorm possible approaches.

**Step 3.** Develop an action plan.

**Step 4.** Set deadlines.

**Step 5.** Establish criteria for evaluation.

**Step 6.** Facilitate action.

**Step 7.** Follow through.

(Note that these are tasks for you as coach, not for employees.)

Does this seem like overkill, too much structure to apply to a small problem? You'll have to be the judge. You won't need all these steps in every situation, and you'll use this process informally when the situation warrants. But be careful about skipping steps, especially the first few times you try it. This method has been tested, and it works.

To best explain the process, we'll use a case study.

Your company has gotten too big for its parking lot, and the informal rule of "survival of the quickest" has started to create a lot of problems.

The lot behind the building used to be more than adequate for all employees. Those who got there earliest got the best spots, closest to the door, but late arrivals still had plenty of spaces to choose from.

> **Don't Skip Step One**
>
> The most common problem-solving mistake? If your attempt at solving a problem runs aground, chances are it's because you skipped the first step. Most folks start deciding what to do before they clearly define and limit the task.

The workforce has expanded, but the parking lot hasn't. Street parking is metered, and you're losing a lot of worker hours while folks run out to feed the meters. Those who get wrapped up in their work invariably find their windshields littered with violation notices. So there's a lot of grumbling. You're also getting complaints about double parking and cars blocking other cars in the lot.

The city is about to impose a two-hour limit on all the meters, and a new strip mall is opening two blocks away, so the problem will only get worse.

You decide to call in your top lieutenant, Fran Quigley, and turn the problem over to her. Rather than just dumping the mess on her desk and walking away, you'll walk her through the seven-step process to ensure a successful solution and to develop her confidence and competence as a problem solver.

## Step 1: Name the Challenge and Describe the Desired Outcome

The way you name the challenge determines in large part how you'll try to solve it—and your chances of succeeding.

**Top lieutenant** The origin of this term makes it a good choice here, despite its military use. It comes from the French words *lieu* and *tenir*, meaning "place" and "to hold." So a "lieutenant" is a place-holder, someone who takes your place when you're unable to do something. That doesn't have to be the same person for every task. In fact, as coach you should spread out special responsibilities among willing employees, depending on your needs and their abilities. (Sometimes you might even choose a lieutenant because he or she needs to develop in a certain area, such as people skills or sense of organization.)

In this case, you might attribute the parking lot congestion to

- too many cars,
- too few available parking spaces,
- poor building location,
- inadequate public transportation,
- an idiotic city council,
- uncooperative worker-commuters, and/or
- timing (everybody wants and needs to park at the same time).

These might all be problems—or valid ways of naming the same problem. The point here is to view the situation from as many perspectives as possible.

You may not be able to do anything about some of them

### Define the Problem

Many people—including a lot of managers—tend to underestimate the importance of this step. After all, when everybody recognizes there's a problem, the only thing left to do is to come up with solutions. Right?

Wrong! That's the best shortcut to a bad solution. This is one time when it pays off to dwell on the negative. In fact, you might even want to take an hour or so to walk around asking for input from employees who drive to work. It's a quick way to get a variety of perspectives, so that you can better understand the problem.

(inadequate public transportation, poor building location, idiotic city council), at least not soon. And you need a solution to the parking mess now.

Staggering work hours might help the problem. In fact, management has discussed that possibility, along with flex time, job sharing, and working from home as ways of improving productivity and employee morale. But you've been told that any change is at least a year away.

So you're left with the basic problem of too many cars trying to fit into too few spaces. Which do you want to attack, the surplus of cars or the lack of spaces?

You come up with the following description of the desired solution:

*Eliminate parking congestion by developing alternatives to single-passenger car commuting among company employees.*

You're ready for Step 2.

## Step 2: Brainstorm Possible Approaches

Remember the two basic principles for effective brainstorming:

Uncouple the idea from the person offering the idea. You're Fran's boss, but in a brainstorming session, you're equals.

Don't judge any idea until you've listed all the options you can come up with.

After you and Fran spend a little time shooting out ideas, you come up with four potential approaches, with a few variations on each:

- Stronger enforcement to eliminate double parking and the use of the lot by non-employees—threats, fines, towing
- Car pools—voluntary? mandatory?
- Encouragement of alternative transportation—bike "club," covered bike rack, discount bus passes
- Assigned parking spaces—by seniority? by distance driven from work? by job classification?

Now it's time to discuss, sort, and judge those possible approaches. You rule out enforcement almost immediately. Not only would it have little effect on the underlying problem of too many cars for too few spaces, but it would create new problems, in terms of employee resentment and frustration. Why punish employees for trying to cope with a situation that's beyond their control?

Mandatory car pools carry the same potential for backlash and raise the problem of enforcement. What's the "or else" for the worker who refuses to share a car? Besides, what happens to employees who regularly stay late to finish a project? If they're required to pool, you lose their flexibility and maybe undermine their commitment to doing a better job.

Trying to encourage voluntary car pooling sounds like a good plan, especially since almost everybody comes and goes at the same times. You could map employee residences by sectors of the city and create sign-up lists to help make car pools easier to create and maintain.

Although both you and Fran like the idea of encouraging voluntary car pooling, you continue to discuss other options.

Before investing time and money in the possibility of encouraging employees to commute by bike—at least in the warmer months—you decide to include a worker survey in the next in-house newsletter, asking how many employees own bikes, live within feasible biking distance, and would consider biking to work. Of course, you also need to allow for physical inabilities (some employees might be unable to ride a bike) and safety (some of the streets leading to your site are quite busy, a situation that will get worse with the new mall). Also, some employees would probably look less professional after biking several miles on a warm summer morning.

You also decide to check with the city transportation department regarding the possibility of getting discount bus ticket books for employees and to check with upper management on the possibility of the company subsidizing all or part of the cost of the passes.

What about assigning parking spaces? That idea seems bad from any angle. In fact, when Fran offered it during brainstorming, you had to fight the urge to reject it. "Just write it down," you reminded yourself. "Don't judge. Not yet."

In light of the company's commitment to bottom-up management and the elimination of caste systems in the workplace, assigned spaces would be a step backward in the move toward greater equality. But an off-hand remark during the ensuing discussion makes you glad you didn't reject the idea too soon.

"Whatever system we work out," Fran said, laughing, "we'll have to deal with those idiotic delivery vans."

Good point. Despite your company's best attempts at diplomacy with the drivers, delivery vans are constantly angled across two spaces, blocking doors and walkways or keeping employees from driving out for lunch.

"Let's assign them spaces someplace in the next county," you suggest.

Then the bulb lights above Fran's head: "How about a loading zone, right out in front of the building?"

"If the city would agree to create a 15-minute area ...."

"We'd get the vans out of the lot. That would help some."

After just a few minutes of focused brainstorming, followed by a little critical analysis, you and Fran have come up with a number of possible approaches to the perplexing parking problem. You're feeling pretty good about yourselves.

Now it's time to get back to work, right?

Not quite.

Quit now, and in a couple of weeks, you'll be wondering why nothing got done about the parking mess. Spend a few more minutes now taking the next steps, and you'll be well on your way to eliminating the problem.

> ### It's OK to Be Dumb
>
> **TRICKS OF THE TRADE**
>
> The worst ideas—the dumbest, most irresponsible, unworkable ones, the ones said in jest, the stand-up-comic kind of ideas—often trigger really creative ideas, the ones that work. That's why you don't want to reject anything during brainstorming. Just keep them coming, keep building on them, keep playing with them, and see what develops.

## Step 3: Develop an Action Plan

Create a simple "to do" list. Next to each task, note who'll take responsibility for making sure it gets done. For the parking problem, the list might look like this:

1. Mark employee residences on an area map. (Fran's assistant, Gerald.)
2. Hang the map in the work room with car pool sign-up lists. (Gerald.)
3. Put an article in the in-house newsletter talking up the benefits of car pooling. (Fran.)
4. Create a survey to determine to what extent employees are able and willing to consider biking to work. (Fran.)
5. Check with the city transportation department about getting discount bus tickets. (Me.)
6. Check with the city and upper management about the possibility of establishing a 15-minute delivery zone in front of the building. (Me.)
7. Get the subject of bus subsidies on the agenda for the next management meeting. (Me.)

You're almost done. Go on to Step 4.

### Contract Deadlines

**Smart Managing** A big advantage to setting deadlines is that it saves time and worry. If you just make a mental note to take care of something, you're likely to think about it from time to time and worry about getting around to it. That can distract you from your other responsibilities. Plus, the more you worry about a task, the more likely you are to put it off and then finally to do it quickly, just to get it off your mind.

So, think of setting deadlines as signing a contract with your project partners.

## Step 4: Set Deadlines

Don't duck the all-important question of "When?" Without a specific deadline, a task may never become a priority, so it may never get done—or it may be done in haste, when somebody thinks to ask about it. Set a deadline for each item on the "to do" list. Better still, write down exactly when you intend to do the task.

## Step 5: Establish Criteria for Evaluation

Make sure you know exactly what outcomes you want and
how you'll know when you get them.

Your major focus is the car pooling. So, you need to
answer some questions. How many people need to start sharing rides for the program to be a success? How will you know
they're actually doing it? Don't get off the track here by thinking that "20 percent is a good participation rate for anything in
this company" or "we'd be doing well to get 100 employees
involved." Think in terms of your goal. Will 20 percent be
enough? More to the point, how many cars will those 100
employees be sharing? 50? 30? 25? How much will that
improve the parking situation? And how much will you need to
count on bikes and buses?

## Step 6: Facilitate Action

What can you as manager do to help employees succeed?
You've already gotten involved by taking on the tasks most
appropriate for you. Consider, too, anything Fran might need
to help her get her tasks done. Maybe you could

give her a few quotes for
her article, to show that
management is supportive
and involved in solving
the parking problem. How
about Gerald? Would he
like you to informally talk
with the employees and
encourage them to sign
up to car pool?

## Step 7: Follow Through

Set a time to get back
together with Fran for a
progress report. The idea

**CAUTION!**

### Help, Don't Intrude

The operative word
here is "facilitate," which means "to
make it easier." Avoid the temptation
to help too much. Some managers
tend to intrude, to assume that the
assigned employee wants help. That's a
bad assumption—and often dangerous. There are times when it might
seem best to just take over a task.
That's paternalistic managing and
about as far away from coaching as
you can get.

Let employees know that you're
there if they need you. But leave that
decision to them.

isn't to create an endless chain of meetings to follow up on meetings. (We all know how that tends to bog down any project!) But you need to ensure accountability, to keep well-intentioned plans from getting lost in the day-to-day shuffle and the crisis of the moment. It's a way of collaboratively enforcing the deadlines. Also, employees who might be hesitant to come talk with you about questions or concerns are more likely to bring them up when they report on their progress.

The first three steps took a bit of explanation, but they aren't difficult, and you don't need to take a lot of time doing them. But they're essential.

Steps 4 through 7 don't even take long to talk about, and they don't take long to do, either. Put your time into focused, shared problem solving at the front end, and the process will pay you back in results and in excellent employee performance. It's not magic. It's just good coaching.

## The Coach's Checklist for Chapter 12

❏ If you want to make sure things get done, you need a methodology, a process for making things happen.

❏ Step one in making things happen: Name the challenge and describe the desired outcome. Don't forget to define it accurately.

❏ Step two: Brainstorm possible approaches. Don't forget to encourage people to be open and maybe even a little outrageous. It triggers creativity.

❏ Step three: Develop an action plan. It's like a to-do list.

❏ Step four: Set deadlines. They provide a sense of urgency.

❏ Step five: Establish criteria for evaluation. Then you'll know if you've succeeded.

❏ Step six: Facilitate action. Figure out what help your employees need to successfully complete their tasks.

❏ Step seven: Follow through. Make sure what's supposed to happen by your deadlines does happen.

# Once More, with Feedback

**"H**ow am I doin'?"

It's one of the most natural questions in the world. We all wonder how others judge us, whether they like or approve of us in a social setting and whether our performance measures up in the workplace. Just because we're too cool to ask doesn't mean we still don't want and need to know.

What if someone very significant in your life, someone with the power to determine your future, gave you feedback on your performance only once each year, and then only in a general way. Ridiculous, right? And yet, many people work day in and day out without any meaningful feedback other than an annual performance review, which is too often only a perfunctory exercise in paper shuffling.

How about the people who work with you? Are you giving them regular, meaningful feedback on their work? If not, you're missing one of the best coaching opportunities—and a great chance to help improve performance.

## Elements of Effective Feedback

The ability to offer effective feedback is essential to the coaching process. Let's look at some of the elements of the most effective feedback a coach can offer.

## Positive, Negative, and Neutral Comments

"I only hear from him when I screw up."

"I close 99 sales in a row, and I don't hear a murmur from the front office. But the minute I let one slip away, all hell breaks loose."

"Sometimes I wonder if I ever do anything right around here!"

Do any of these comments sound familiar? If not, then you're working in the only ideal company in the country.

For too many workers, "feedback" means only "criticism." But constant criticism is seldom effective in coaching workers to peak performance and, in fact, may suppress performance as workers labor to hide their mistakes and to avoid contact with supervisors.

**Key Term** **Feedback** The return of information about the result of a process or activity. This is a term from general systems theory. Technically, it refers to information about the outputs or functioning of a system that is used to maintain system performance or to control a system or process.

That sounds very mechanical. Certainly no manager, especially a coach, wants to treat employees as if they were components in a system. After all, they're human beings, not machines. But with machines at least you get feedback *continually*, both *negative* and *positive*.

Negative feedback is only one aspect of the total range of responses to a worker's efforts. Feedback should include praise for work well done and for honest effort that fails to yield results through no fault of the worker. Often, a worker just needs to hear about the unseen results of her efforts, a simple reporting of outcomes with neither criticism nor praise attached.

## Timeliness

"Remember that presentation you made last June? You know,

the pitch to the buyers from McConnell? I thought it was very effective. Right on target. Nice going."

Compliments are great any time. But the further the compliment becomes separated from the deed, the less emotional impact it will have. The recipient of the compliment might even doubt your motives.

Likewise, the longer a suggestion for improvement follows performance, the less effect it will have.

"Gee, if I'd known how the boss felt about my McConnell presentation, I would have felt more confident when I did my presentation for the Archer account a month later—and maybe we would have won that account."

---

### Give My Best to Sparky

You'll likely make some big mistakes if you just think big.

Smart managers think in terms of the big picture, of the company as a system, of teamwork. But they don't neglect the individuals.

If possible, walk around the workplace regularly, providing feedback—especially positive feedback—to each employee.

If that's impossible, how about electronic mail? It's easy enough to write up a quick message, then send it off in seconds. If you're tempted to send out a form memo to all the members of a team, take just a few minutes more to make it an e-mail, which you can customize for each individual. Maybe just add a comment like "Give my best to your dog, Sparky" or "By the way, I hope Meg is enjoying soccer." It's a great chance to show how well you know the employees. (And it just might encourage you to get to know them better!)

---

Whether it's negative or positive or (most likely) both, link your feedback as closely as possible to the behavior you're commenting on.

### Individual Recognition

Employees take pride in playing on an effective team and share in the reflected glory of a team victory.

But that doesn't mean that employees don't appreciate

recognition for their individual efforts and achievements in the team's success. Quite the contrary!

That's why a form memo addressed to "members of the task force committee" doesn't mean nearly as much as a personal note to each individual on the committee, even if each member of the group gets one—as long as the notes don't say exactly the same thing.

Likewise, general comments about "poor overall performance" to a group of workers will have little effect on any one member of that group. It's human nature to ascribe low team achievement to the other guy or to "bad chemistry."

---

### Know What You're Praising

Marilyn was a wonderful person, and she wanted to be a wonderful vice president. So, she'd take a few moments from time to time to walk around and chat with the employees.

She emphasized the positive, saying such things as "Good job there!" and "Hey, I like the way we're all working together!" The employees appreciated her comments, but they all knew that she was clueless about how any individual was actually performing—and sometimes even about what a certain worker was assigned to do.

The moral of the story: praise is good, but specific praise means much more and is far more effective.

---

## Specific Examples

The best way to individualize feedback is to refer to specific, unique behaviors.

Which comment would seem more credible to you if you read it in a letter of recommendation for a potential hire—a series of general references to the worker being "dependable" and a "self-starter" or specific examples of projects that worker carried out effectively and independently?

Specific examples carry more weight every time.

The same goes for any feedback you give on job performance. Refer to specific actions and outcomes. Otherwise, even praise sounds empty.

### Sincerity

Say what you mean, mean what you say, and say it like you mean it.

Sincerity is equal parts speaking your truth and speaking it honestly. Your feedback must be genuine, and you must deliver it in a way that is natural and comfortable for you.

Empty praise is no more effective than chronic carping. Employees soon learn to screen out and disregard both.

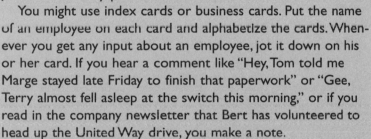

### Keep Track of Good Work

If you manage a large number of employees or if you just have memory problems, take notes.

You might use index cards or business cards. Put the name of an employee on each card and alphabetize the cards. Whenever you get any input about an employee, jot it down on his or her card. If you hear a comment like "Hey, Tom told me Marge stayed late Friday to finish that paperwork" or "Gee, Terry almost fell asleep at the switch this morning," or if you read in the company newsletter that Bert has volunteered to head up the United Way drive, you make a note.

Then, take the next opportunity to compliment Marge and Bert or express your concern to Terry. Just glance at the card to refresh your memory, and you're ready to go.

And you shouldn't try to adopt a "management style" when delivering feedback. The best style for you is your own natural manner of speaking and acting, without forced mannerisms or studied inflections.

What's the best way to be natural? Practice!

That may seem contradictory, but it makes sense. Here's a suggestion. When you're at home, make a point of stopping in front of the mirror and complimenting yourself. It may seem silly at first. But study your reflection. How do you look? How do you sound? Sincere? Natural?

Work at being yourself. Just a minute or two from time to

time can make a big difference in your style—and make your feedback to employees more effective.

(By the way, that natural style is what we chose for this book. We could have used a "management style," but we believe that a more natural style just works better for more effective communication. What do you think?)

## Before You Deliver Feedback...

Before letting someone know how he or she is doing, take a few moments to gather your thoughts and decide on the best way to deliver your message. The guidelines discussed in this section will help you make that decision.

- **Think before you speak**. What? How? Why?
  Effective feedback takes preparation. Think about what you want to say, how you want to say it, and what effect you intend for it to have. It's best not to just blurt out feedback.

  But feedback must also be timely, right? We're not talking about a month-long deliberation here. Preparation time for effective feedback is often minutes or even seconds, but it's important that you take those seconds to consider what, how, and why.

- **Say it face-to-face.** You no doubt have to fill out performance reports, write memos, and create many types of written evaluations of your employees. Creating a paper trail is a necessary evil in the workplace. But reports, memos, and written evaluations rarely match the effectiveness of the spoken word, delivered in person. Don't hide behind paper or the telephone or e-mail. If possible, say it with your presence as well as your words.

- **Go one-on-one**. Two is feedback. Three's a performance. The presence of witnesses alters your message in ways you can't control. Criticism delivered in public isn't feedback; it's punishment. It's also humiliating, and folks don't tend to learn anything helpful while being shamed.

  Praising workers in front of their peers can be a real ego

booster, of course, but for some it can be almost as embarrassing as criticism, as it focuses attention. It may also cause resentment among other workers. Public praise of one may seem like implied criticism of the others. (And, for some, it may dredge up old fears of being scorned by other kids as a "teacher's pet.")

Here's another reason not to go public with individual feedback: you're only human. Whether you're delivering good news or bad, you'll naturally tend to aim that delivery at least in part at the audience. Playing to the crowd may be human nature, but it's a lousy feedback technique.

> **"Praise in Public, Criticize in Private"**    Smart Managing
>
> That bit of folk wisdom has guided wise supervisors for ages, and it's still a worthy guide in many situations. You'll have to judge when public praise will serve your overall goal of coaching for peak performance. Just be aware of the potential dangers.

## Delivering Bad News

How do you feel about delivering bad news? If you're like most managers, you may feel that it's the part of your job that takes the most out of you.

You can't avoid it, of course. If you try to dodge the responsibility, you're just likely to make matters worse—and to develop a reputation that will make you less effective. But you can certainly learn how to handle a bad news situation.

Above all, you need to avoid an adversarial tone. Setting up a boss-employee confrontation will only create resistance and resentment, not better work. Let's look at some ways to deliver bad news effectively.

1. **Select an appropriate environment.** The setting may be as important as the message. Where you choose to deliver that message becomes part of the communication.

Consider using the employee's own space—office, cubicle, or work station—so long as it's private. Playing the feedback game on the worker's home court strips you of the trappings

### The Round Table

**Smart Managing** "First among peers." That was the title of the person who may have been the first manager-coach in history, King Arthur.

Sure, he was the king, the CEO of his country. But when he met with his knights, his employees, he made sure to emphasize equality. He didn't sit on his throne. He didn't stand over them or make them drop to their knees. And he certainly did not seek shelter behind a tree stump.

He gathered his employees around a table that had no head, no place of honor, no physical sign that he was their superior. That team was known as the Knights of the Round Table and King Arthur gained a reputation for leading his teammates as "first among peers."

That approach, fit for a king, is certainly fit for any manager.

of power, which means that the roar of your authority won't drown out your words. Employees tend to feel more relaxed in their own area and thus are a little less likely to become easily inflamed.

If you decide instead to call the employee into your office, invite him or her to sit down and then resist the temptation to remain standing (elevating yourself while diminishing the employee), to sit on your "throne" (a better, higher chair), or to retreat behind your desk or other barrier.

You might also select a neutral site. If so, be sure to choose a pleasant place, not a public thoroughfare where you're likely

### **CAUTION!**

### Don't Stall

"Drawing on shared purpose" doesn't mean a long oration on the history of the organization or a thorough review of the mission statement. It probably doesn't even mean talking on at length about how all members of the staff are working hard together toward a common goal.

A little small talk may, of course, help to relax both of you. But the longer you delay coming to the point, the more tension you'll create. Employees know you didn't call them in to talk about the weather.

to be interrupted or a messy storage area.

**2. Talk from common goals.** Draw on your shared purpose, the goals that unite you in the work you do. Ultimately, you both want the same thing (peak performance). Explain how you intend your comments to serve that purpose.

### Be Reasonable!

Smart
Managing

You're the boss! Why do you need to give reasons for your decisions, especially to an employee who's been performing poorly or behaving badly?

Consider it an investment in your employees and in yourself.

Think about it. Even if you decide to terminate this employee, everybody will know how you handled the situation. And whether or not they believe you made the right decision to punish or even to terminate that employee, they'll wonder whether you'll stop being a reasonable, fair manager if any of them happens to cross some line. In other words, they're likely to identify with that one employee, and that reaction could hurt your work culture.

Handling this situation in a fair and reasonable way allows you the opportunity to really put to the test your commitment to being an effective coach and a smart manager.

**3. Offer reasons.** It isn't so just because you say it's so.

This exchange isn't an inquisition. You aren't a prosecuting attorney, marshalling evidence to win a conviction, nor are you a logician, "proving" a point.

But you are the boss, and as boss, you bear the burden of explaining why you've reached the conclusion that an employee's performance is lacking or that his or her behavior is inappropriate. Explain the "why" as you deliver the "what."

**4. Speak to their needs.** You've got your reasons for speaking. What are their reasons for listening?

How will your comments help them do their jobs better? How will that improved performance help them grow and possibly advance?

If you don't have ready answers to these questions, think about them first. You'll provide more useful information, and you'll stand a much better chance of getting the results you want.

Ask yourself, "What's in this for them?" before you speak.

**5. Talk about actions, not motives**. You're a coach, not a therapist or a parole officer. You're coaching performance, not personality. Confine your message to what they do, not who they are.

You don't really know who they are. As a supervisor, you must gather enough information to accurately judge how they perform. But any conclusions about the motives behind that performance are most likely just speculation.

Inappropriate comment: "You're lazy."

Appropriate comment: "You've missed your quota the last two weeks."

Let the worker tell you why—if it's useful to the discussion.

**6. Assume your fair share of responsibility**. The employees didn't follow your instructions. They heard them. They agreed with them (or at least they said they did). But they still didn't carry them out.

Be open to the possibility that you didn't explain clearly what you wanted them to do. It takes two to communicate— not just a willing receiver but also an effective sender. Your message is effective only if it gets the desired result.

"I didn't get the message across" may be a much better way to begin the discussion than "You didn't get the message."

This isn't a matter of being nice. It's a matter of being effective, of not making a bad situation worse.

**7. Provide choices, options, and opportunities**. If you've been clear, compelling, and compassionate in explaining why the worker has missed the mark, it's now time to explain what he or she can and should do to perform better. Remember: your goal here isn't to punish, but to improve performance.

If you have a plan in mind, lay it out and give the worker

the chance to buy into the plan or to modify it. Ask for suggestions. End the session only when both of you know exactly what the worker should do next.

## Feedback on Your Feedback

We began this chapter with one of the most natural questions in the world—"How am I doin'?"

Employees need to know the answer to that question, and you need to know whether you're doing your job well, too.

The best way to judge how effectively you're communicating with employees is, of course, to observe their subsequent performance. But you can benefit from more mmedi-

>
> **Ask, Don't Challenge**
>
> "Have I made myself clear?"
>
> By that question you mean "Have I been effective in communicating my point?"
>
> But the employee may hear "Did you get that, dumbo?"
>
> It all depends on the context and your tone and expression. Make sure your question is truly a question, and not a challenge.

ate feedback on your feedback. Here are some ways to get it.

- **Keep the conversation open-ended.** Don't lecture. Encourage dialog. Use receptive body language—arms down at your sides rather than crossed over your chest, for example. Pause frequently so that employees can reply without having to interrupt. (Some people are very reluctant to interrupt others, especially if it's the boss.)
- **Ask questions.** Asking an employee for an opinion or observation does not in any way diminish your authority. If anything, it enhances it. If you want to know, ask. However, if you don't want to hear the answer, don't ask the question.

"Tell me what you really think" can mean what it says. It can also mean "Tell me that you agree with me."

Don't ask because you think it's the right thing to do. Don't ask because you read in a management book that you're supposed to. You may only trick the employee into beginning a conversation you don't want to have. And if you then show no interest in the reply, the employee may feel betrayed. If you work hard at building trust, don't undermine your efforts by betraying that trust, even unintentionally.

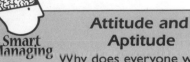

**Attitude and Aptitude**

**Smart Managing** Why does everyone want to know more, but nobody wants to be a "know-it-all"?

The answer to that riddle is "P."

Confused? Well, the difference between knowing more and being a know-it-all is the difference between *aptitude* and *attitude*. The more you know, the greater your aptitude. But if you act like you know it all, that's an attitude—and it will keep you from learning.

Be open about your ignorance. You don't know everything. Don't pretend you do.

Information should flow in both directions. You'll enhance your authority and assure your employees that you want to be fair by asking for input when you need it.

Accept employees' comments without judgment. The words "You're welcome to your opinion" shouldn't be followed by "but ...." They also shouldn't be dripping with scorn or sarcasm.

First, all employees are entitled to their opinions, whether you agree with them or not, whether you like them or not. Second, if you show that you're not really open to their comments, you're going to get fewer and fewer of them. Employees won't risk a cold reception (although some may relish the chance to put a thorn in your side).

Don't get defensive, and don't get drawn into an argument. Nobody ever wins that kind of battle, and an argument *will* undermine your authority. Accept contrary opinions. Agree to disagree as to causes or blame. But then reaffirm exactly what you want the employee to do and how you expect it done.

You're not infallible. You're not all-knowing. But you are the boss. That title is certainly no guarantee of perfection, but it does mean that you're responsible for your team of employees. In fact, that's what Harry S. Truman meant when he said, "The buck stops here." A good manager doesn't claim to be infallible or all-knowing. A good manager just recognizes where the buck stops.

Feedback is essential to effective coaching. Good feedback is personal and sincere and, like all coaching behaviors, intended to foster peak performance.

## The Coach's Checklist for Chapter 13

❑ Feedback is important. If you want your employees to know how they're doing, you have to tell them.

❑ Don't just tell employees when they've made a mistake. Make sure you deliver positive feedback as well. That's how your employees will know what you like. And make your feedback timely, as well.

❑ Praise the team, but don't forget that individuals like praise for their individual achievements as well.

❑ Make sure your feedback is specific. General feedback doesn't mean much.

❑ Be sincere. Say what you mean, mean what you say, and say it like you mean it.

❑ Before you deliver feedback ... think before you speak; say it face-to-face, and go one-on-one.

❑ Know how to deliver bad news. Don't make it a confrontation.

# Coaching by Rewarding

Reward the performance you want.

It sounds so simple, and yet many managers fail to follow this basic principle. Most often, managers seem to ignore competence and focus attention only on performance or behaviors they don't like.

When that happens, it may discourage peak performance, if employees decide that there's not much incentive to do better than meet the standards. And you're going to be spending a lot of time correcting, criticizing, and even punishing. That's not a happy prospect.

So, it's important to know about coaching by rewards.

Let's take a look at the three basic kinds of rewards you can use to encourage peak performance: tangible, symbolic, and intangible.

## Tangible Rewards

Thanks to an exuberant actor named Cuba Gooding Jr., the phrase "Show me the money!" shot from novelty to catch phrase to cliché to parody (all in the space of about a week, it seemed). This was because it so perfectly expressed an almost universally held sentiment: if you want my best effort and my loyalty, pay me big dollars.

Money is certainly the most tangible of tangible rewards for peak performance in the workplace. But what some managers don't realize is that an increase in compensation will serve as a reward for meritorious service only if the raise is clearly linked to the performance and is unique.

### Don't Make Promotions Payoffs

Can a promotion be a mistake? After all, if a person works hard and earns it, it's only fair!

Not necessarily. A promotion can be a very expensive mistake, in two ways.

If employees get the feeling that a promotion is only a payoff and not recognition of their ability to handle more responsibility, they're more likely to do less. So, when you promote an employee, be sure that the promotion is not only a reward, showing thanks, but also a challenge, bestowing new responsibilities.

And the second way in which a promotion can be a mistake? Have you ever heard of the Peter Principle? We all know of instances in which people were promoted to positions beyond their competence.

If everyone in the job classification gets an identical or nearly identical annual "merit" raise—regardless of performance—it simply becomes a step increase. You've rewarded longevity but not specific performance. You're encouraging employees to survive, but not to thrive.

Advancement in rank stands with a raise in pay as a powerful tangible reward. In fact, they're often linked together. During wartime, soldiers could receive rapid advancement as reward for their deeds under fire. Your ability to confer stripes and stars on those on your own little battlefield is much more limited, of course, but the ability to work up the ladder through excellent performance is a powerful inducement.

Money and rank may be the biggest and most obvious tangible rewards, but they're not the only ones. Other effective rewards include time off (from a few hours to a sabbatical) and perks (the proverbial "key to the executive wash room," a reserved parking space, more flexible hours, an office with a window, and box seats at the local sports venue, just to mention a few).

## Symbolic Rewards

This is the category of trophies, trinkets, and toys—tangible items that have little or no monetary value but are invested with symbolic significance, if the giver and the recipient both believe in that value. Such rewards include "Worker of the Week/Month/Year" trophies and plaques, a profile in the in-house newsletter, a picture in the hallway Heroes Gallery, and a mouse pad with company logo. Some of the best symbolic awards are traditional, such as an awards dinner at which employees gather to honor one or more from among them.

> **⚠ CAUTION!**
>
> **Trinket Alert!** Symbolic rewards can easily lose their significance if they're overdone. Don't over-use them or they won't be valuable to the recipients. Don't oversell them or nobody will take them seriously.
>
> You might want to establish several levels of symbolic rewards. Confer the highest rewards in a ceremony that connotes their importance, but keep those to a minimum. Then bestow the lower levels of symbolic rewards with a mixture of goodwill and humor—perhaps with mock seriousness but not real solemnity. Every-one will laugh along with the recipient, while secretly hoping for a turn.

## Intangible Rewards

Most people assume that money is the primary positive motivator for peak performance. But surveys of worker attitudes show money in only fourth or fifth place on the list of motivators. Intangibles like "job satisfaction," "chances to learn," and "independence" consistently take the top spots in the rankings.

Reward workers by trusting them. Give them greater control over their work lives and allow for increased responsibility—so long as you link it with the authority and resources needed to fulfill the new role.

Provide opportunities for workers to increase mastery and skill, to learn and grow, to take ownership of and pride in their work. They'll strive to achieve the rewards that are inherent in the performance itself, independent of your judgment of that performance.

Provide the means and the opportunities. They'll do the rest.

## Rules of Rewarding

There are three simple points to keep in mind when rewarding employees.

### Link the Reward to the Behavior

The reward will reinforce the action only if it comes as a consequence of that action—and employees know it. You can call it a "merit raise" (or anything else you want to), but if it comes for some reason other than meritorious performance, it will either reinforce some other behavior (endurance leading to longevity, most likely) or fail to reinforce anything.

You can link performance and reward in any of several ways:

> **Key Term**
>
> **Promotion** The original meaning was "movement forward," as when soldiers were asked to move ahead of their comrades and assume leadership responsibilities.
>
> Unfortunately, this word is currently used only in terms of positions and titles. Then employees and managers feel limited. ("You've been doing a great job, Catherine, but I can't promote you because there aren't any positions open" or "You're the best of the marketing assistants, but we've already got a director, so how about if we create a title for you, like senior marketing assistant in charge of words?")
>
> An effective coaching manager finds a way to move good employees forward without positions or titles.

- The reward can be given when a worker meets or exceeds established performance standards. For example, "Meet your sales goal and you get your bonus."
- Special merit awards can recognize performance above

existing standards in quantity and/or quality.
- Rewards can derive from completion of the task itself.

### Confer the Reward Fairly

There's no place here for paying off friends or favoring pets. Although you'll never totally escape the subjective element in evaluating performance, you must base merit awards on objective, measurable standards. Production is relatively easy to measure objectively: at the end of the day or the week or the month, you count the number of units manufactured or sold or painted or installed. Strive to objectify your standards as much as possible by offering clear definitions of what "better performance" or "better behavior" means in context.

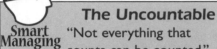

**The Uncountable**

Smart Managing  "Not everything that counts can be counted."

Although it's important to measure what workers do, we should never slip into neglecting the importance of things that are difficult or even impossible to measure, such as team spirit or dedication "above and beyond the call of duty."

Then make sure everyone has equal opportunity to compete for the reward. Create specific performance goals, guidelines, and standards, and then communicate them to all employees. Make sure all employees have the information, the equipment, and the materials they need to do the job.

**Equal Reward Opportunity**

Mistake Proofing  Equal access to the *competition* is not the same thing at all as equal access to the *reward*. "Fair" doesn't mean that over time the rewards will even out, that everybody will get an equal share. All workers must have an equal opportunity to compete for the reward, but the rewards must go to those who earn them. Otherwise, you undermine the merit system.

### Make Sure All Employees Understand About the Rewards

Telling the truth and being believed are two different things. We've all known credible liars and sincere folks whom nobody quite trusts.

Being fair in your allocation of rewards and being seen as fair are also, alas, two different things. You must be fair, and you must be sure everybody knows it.

Communicate and explain performance standards clearly. Announce merit awards publicly. Avoid the appearance as well as the reality of favoritism.

---

### Don't "Tilt" the System

Reward carefully, to avoid the "tilt," the old tendency that "the rich get richer and poor get poorer."

Sometimes you may unintentionally encourage that sort of tilt. For example, if you reward your sales rep of the year with a Lexus, she may gain an advantage that will help her be on top the next year. Or if you reward your best secretary with a faster computer and his own copy machine (yes, those should be tools, not rewards!), then he's likely to be even more efficient and have an edge over the other secretaries.

These are just two totally fictitious examples. But look around you: sometimes the truth is stranger than fiction. A word to the wise: avoid encouraging the tilt.

---

## The Coach as a Cheerleader

In the first chapter, we likened your job as manager or supervisor to that of a coach of an athletic team. A coach's activities—conducting practices, instructing, making out the lineup, planning strategy, calling plays, arguing with the officials on behalf of the players—have their counterparts in your daily activities—training, assigning work, solving problems, giving feedback, arguing with your bosses to get your staff what they need to do the job.

Most good coaches perform one more important function: they root, root, root for the home team—loudly, passionately, and publicly. Coaches may be their players' most vocal critics, but they're also their biggest cheerleaders.

That's you, coach—the best cheerleader your "players" will ever have. Share their triumphs and their concerns. Exhort them to greater performance. Reward them with lavish praise.

> ## Concentrate on Your Players
>
> There have been many college basketball coaches who have compiled winning records. But UCLA coach John Wooden stands out as perhaps the best, because he made the development and growth of his players his first priority While other coaches have stressed winning and sometimes burned out or frustrated their players, Wooden concentrated on his players—and they brought home victory after victory.

Savor their achievements without taking any of the credit away from them.

Many of your employees will never thank you for being a great manager and coach. Some won't even be aware of the extent to which you make their jobs more satisfying and their efforts more productive. But they'll reward you with peak performance (and that's what you wanted all along).

## The Coach's Checklist for Chapter 14

❑ Reward the performance you want.

❑ Tangible rewards provide valuable feedback only if employees connect them to individual performance.

❑ Rules of rewards include (1) link reward to behavior, (2) confer the reward fairly, and (3) make sure all employees understand about rewards.

❑ Be a cheerleader for your team. That's another intangible reward for your team.

# Bonus Principles for Good Coaching (and Good Living)

Here's your reward for reading this far: power principles that will raise you from the ranks of the merely excellent to the brilliant.

### The Principle of Getting Started: It Doesn't Matter Where You Start

It only matters *that* you start.

Action often must precede understanding and almost always comes before certainty.

Don't wait for a problem to develop and grow before you start applying the techniques we've explored in the first 14 chapters. Don't wait to be inspired. Don't wait for insight. Don't wait, period. Start anywhere. Work your way toward inspiration and insight.

On any given project, get involved in your coaching right up front, helping your employees define the problem, develop the approach, and create the action plan. Much better to start out strong and smart and together than to try to untangle the problem later. The time you spend at the front end of the project will return to you twofold in the problems you don't have to solve and the explanations you don't have to make later.

## The Principle of Control: You Can't Control Anybody

You can motivate them. You can direct their energies. You can teach them, lead them, praise them, and guide them.

But you can't control them—and you wouldn't want to if you could. You don't want compliant slaves. You want effective, independent workers.

When you evaluate workers' performance and related workplace behaviors, put your perceptions to this test:

"Is what they're doing *wrong,* or is it just *different?*"

Too many supervisors manage by the "my way or the highway" standard. They generally view differences as a threat to their authority.

You'll waste a lot of time and engender a lot of anger and resentment making people undo and redo things they did fine but different.

Part of your job as a coach is to learn your workers' individual work styles and to allow as much as possible for people to do it their way—as long as you get the result you want, when you want it.

No threats. No chains. Just clear explanations of mutual goals.

## The Principle of Decisions: Make Them—Promptly

"Not to decide is to decide," theologian Harvey Cox said.

If you fail to make a decision, you decide by default. You also abandon your role as leader and turn the fate of your project over to the prevailing wind.

Deciding not to act may be a valid choice. But failing to decide never is. Get as much information as you can. Cast your net wide for possible courses of action. Weigh carefully but quickly. Then decide.

Haste makes waste? Sometimes. But waiting makes nothing. Waste is a natural result of productivity. Throw away the waste, and you're left with your solution.

## The Principle of Time: Don't Waste It

> ### Timely Decisions
>
> **Smart Managing**
>
> "The percentage of mistakes in quick decisions is no greater than in long-drawn-out vacillations," notes Anne O'Hare McCormick, "and the effect of decisiveness itself makes things go and creates confidence."

Don't waste time—yours or theirs. Sure, that's easier said than done. But you can make a big difference by avoiding these pervasive time eaters.

### Memo Mania

Are you sure you have to write it down?

If you really have to write it down—no doubt so that somebody can file it—don't try to make your employees read it unless it's really necessary. And don't assume they know what's in it just because you sent it to them.

Make sure the message is worth the ink and paper, then follow up to make sure employees got it and understand it.

### Info Glut

Computers have made it possible to access virtually any information source in the galaxy—if you can find it. We're all drowning in information, learning to put off decisions while we gather ever more data.

- Don't mistake information for knowledge.
- Don't mistake knowledge for wisdom.
- Don't mistake wisdom for an informed decision that gets the project moving.

Just because you can get the information doesn't mean you have to get it. Apply commonsense, reasonable guidelines, and set a time limit for "surfing the 'Net."

### Meeting Menace

People don't hate meetings.

They hate nonsense. They hate wasting their time. They

hate listening to someone read a list of announcements to them, when they could have selectively read (and skipped) them much faster themselves. And they really loathe spending a precious hour discussing an issue that matters to them, only to find out that a decision has already been made.

Hold meetings only for necessary interactions that can't take place any other way. Plan every meeting by setting an agenda. Circulate discussion items and needed information ahead of time. And run meetings tightly.

### Multiple Management

To the extent that you have the power to make it happen, make sure workers report to one and only one supervisor for any given project. Having to report to two bosses is a sure time-waster. Define lines of responsibility and authority clearly and publicly. Don't pass the management buck, and don't let anybody else pass it, either.

### Marilyn Monroe Complex

Don't make people wait. It's bad manners, and it's inefficient and ineffective managing.

Don't make an appointment you can't keep. Don't show up late for any meeting, especially if you're going to be running it. Don't make anybody wait on the phone while you take another call.

Making people wait wastes their time—and it insults them. It conveys the clear message that you consider what you're doing to be a lot more important than interacting with them.

If you can't help being late, make sure you apologize to the group, quickly and sincerely. If you must explain, keep it short.

### Trivial Pursuit

Effective time managers learn to ask themselves the Lakein Question (named for Alan Lakein, the progenitor of modern time management techniques): "Do I want or need to be doing this right now?"

Ask this question on behalf of employees, too. Don't give them something to do just so that they'll have something to do. That's how adults treat children—and it's a quick way to send a strong message about how you really view your employees.

Yes, the word "business" means the state of being busy— but there's no profit in simply keeping busy. Take the time to create meaningful work plans, as you coach employees toward being independent self-starters who solve problems without you.

### TBM

TBM stands for Total Bull Movement, and it's sweeping the nation. Don't get caught up in it.

Resist movements, slogans, acronyms, management models, and other "revolutionary" approaches that require hours of organization and training, many dollars of consultant time, a new file for the records, and a new employee to enter all the data for those records.

Instead, treat these movements and models as perspectives that can help you better understand how to improve your management style, rather than as ideologies that will only narrow your thinking. The wise manager is one who is slow to embrace or to reject a new approach, but eager to learn from it.

## The Principle of Questions: Ask Lots of Them

No such thing as a dumb question? Nonsense. You can ask lots of dumb questions, dumb in the sense that you really should have known the answer. Perhaps you did know it at one time and just forgot.

What's the worst thing that could happen if you ask a dumb question? You'll reveal your ignorance, which may be a little embarrassing, an occasional price to pay for not being perfect. Now, what's the worst thing that could happen if you fail to ask

> **Ask to Find Out**
>
> The best way to avoid mistakes is to ask questions. As Malcolm Forbes once observed, "One who never asks either knows everything or knows nothing." He also noted that "the smart ones ask when they don't know—and sometimes when they do."

questions? You remain ignorant.

The answers to a lot of questions may seem obvious, but they often help us gain insight and initiate creative break-throughs.

## The Principle of Mistakes: Everyone Makes Them

Admit them. Fix them. Learn from them. Move on.

The folks who work with you know you're human. They'll have a lot more confidence in you when you show them that you know it, too.

If the notion of making a mistake still bothers you, call it something else. Call it learning.

The story of Thomas Alva Edison and the light bulb is worth retelling in this context. Edison tried hundreds of materials, trying to find a filament that would heat up when an electric current passed through it, giving off light without burning up. After hundreds of disappointments, there was still no guarantee that the idea would ever work.

When asked how he was able to endure so many failures, Edison reportedly said that he hadn't considered any of his attempts to be failures. He was simply learning what wouldn't work.

> **Smart Managing**
>
> **Turn Failure into Success**
>
> "Failure is success if we learn from it."
> That inspirational reminder comes not from a philosopher who doesn't understand business, but from Malcolm Forbes.

Mistakes teach us what doesn't work. That's very valuable information.

When you fall short of your goal, learn and go on. Redefine your goal, alter your approach, and get help. As long as you continue to try, you can never fail.

## The Principle of Anger: Feel It—Don't Act on It

A worker screws up and you lash out, administering a vicious, public reprimand.

It's only natural. You're righteously mad. All your hard work is wasted in a stupid, careless second. The worker had it coming.

Besides, if you try to bottle up all that anger, you're courting a heart attack or a stroke. Let it all out. Vent that spleen. It's better for you, right?

Feeling anger—along with frustration and disappointment—is natural. But you don't have to let the feeling control your actions. Ride out the adrenaline rush with a few deep breaths and some calm self-talk. If you can't handle the situation yet, walk away until you can. Then do the right thing, instead of the natural thing.

Anger, if not restrained, is frequently more harmful than the wrong that provoked it. That sentence is as true now as it was when Seneca spoke it two thousand years ago. You can't undo a mistake. But if you let it make you act in anger, you're probably just going to make the situation worse.

## The Principle of Objectivity: There's No Such Thing

Managers are supposed to be objective, to view the situation without emotion, to judge dispassionately, to rule infallibly.

Don't believe it!

You don't check your humanity at the door when you show up for work in the morning. You bring all of you to the task—your knowledge and experience, your empathy and understanding, your ambition and disappointment, your opinions and prejudices.

You're going to like some workers more than others.

You'll find some a lot easier to talk with. You'll appreciate those who seem most cooperative, most in tune with your philosophy and your ways of doing things, while

> **Objectivity** Focused on the facts, without feelings. That may be a good approach for scientists studying rocks or bacteria, but for a manager working with people, objectivity can seriously limit interactions and constrain relationships. A manager who believes in being objective with employees is likely to be less effective.

resenting those who seem to fight you every step of the way.

In short, you'll respond to people as a person. And that means you'll be subjective.

Don't hide your biases from yourself. Own up to them and then compensate for these "natural" feelings to be sure you're being fair to all employees—whether you particularly like them or not.

## The Principle of Generalization: Be Specific

Have you ever endured a long explanation from a boss, only to leave even more confused about what you're supposed to do next?

Learn from that experience. When you explain the new project, remember that the fundamental question every employee wants and needs answered is simply this: "What am I supposed to do?"

Here's a simple test to ensure you answer it. Make sure the instruction has a verb in it. The verb "to be" in any of its forms doesn't count. Include an action verb in your explanation.

## The Principle of Small Stuff: Don't Sweat It

Conventional wisdom has this one half right.

You don't have enough physical, emotional, and psychic energy to squander on the dozens of daily crises that nip at you in the workplace. Keep your perspective, your priorities, and your balance.

Your decisions really do matter—for your organization, the people who work with you, and your own sense of integrity and worth. You'll face lots of big challenges that deserve all the sweat, all the concern and thought and effort you can give them. Just make sure you've got enough in reserve when these challenges come.

## The Principle of Fear: Face It

Stop running, the Chinese proverb advises, and face the monster that is chasing you. When you do, you often find that the monster isn't so monstrous after all.

Fear needn't cripple you. Courage is, after all, acting in the face of your fear, not in the absence of any fear. But trying to avoid the confrontation that frightens you just makes you incapable of right action. If you don't face your fears, you allow them greater power over you.

Don't fear the fear. It can't hurt you. In fact, when you're able to focus it, fear can keep you alert and give you energy.

Feel your fear. Then do the right thing anyway.

## The Principle of Role Modeling: Coach by Example

The workplace needs clear lines of authority, well-defined responsibility, and accountability for actions done and not done.

You want respect from your workers. Respect them.

You want them to listen to you. Listen to them.

You want them to withhold criticism when brainstorming for solutions to problems. Then stifle yours.

You've got to walk your talk, coach. Treat them exactly as you would have them treat you. That rule truly is golden, and it's the smartest advice on human relations you can ever give or get.

## The Principle of Life: You Need One

You are not your job. Your ultimate worth is not in your work. You don't have to earn the right to exist.

Devote time and energy to your life outside of work. It will make you a better worker. But even if it doesn't, it will give you a sense of satisfaction, contentment, and joy.

Nobody ever said, "I wish I'd spent more time at the office."

What if you died tomorrow? What would you most regret never having done?

OK. Now go do it!

Now you know everything you need to know to be an effective coach. For that matter, you probably knew virtually all of it when you started reading this book. You may have never seen it all put down in one place before, and you may have needed to have your own good instincts confirmed in print.

But coaching isn't just about knowing. It's about doing. *Coach* now stops being a noun, a name for your relationship with your workers, and becomes a verb, the way you interact with those workers every day.

## The Coach's Checklist for Chapter 15

❏  Go back and review the points in this chapter. They'll work for you on the job and, yes, in your life off the job as well.

# Index